Frames of Time

A Journey Through Cinematic Evolution

by Brussel Stevens

Dear Esteemed Reader,

Thank you immensely for choosing this book to join your collection. We imagine that you've already embarked on an exploration of ideas within these pages, and we couldn't be happier about it!

Now, if you find yourself chuckling, pondering, or even debating with the words in front of you, we'd absolutely love to hear about it. If you can spare a few moments to pen down your thoughts in a review, we would be as delighted as a dictionary on a spelling bee!

An Amazon review would be excellent - but hey, we're far from picky. Whether it's a scribble on the back of a grocery list, a tweet, or even a message in a bottle (though that might take a while to reach us), your feedback is gold.

Writing a review might not be as fun as a spontaneous dance-off, but we promise it'll bring grins to our faces, warmth to our hearts, and incredibly valuable insights to future readers.

With Gratitude,

Bo Bennett, PhD
Publisher
Archieboy Holdings, LLC.

Table of Contents

Introduction

Cinematography is an ever-evolving art form that transcends time and technology, shaping the way we see and experience films. In "Frames of Time," we will embark on a fascinating journey through the rich history and future possibilities of cinematic visual storytelling. From the silent masterpieces of the early 20th century to the latest innovations in virtual reality, this book offers a comprehensive exploration of the techniques, styles, and visionaries that have shaped the world of cinema. Through insights into foundational principles, iconic films, and cutting-edge advancements, readers will gain an in-depth understanding of the art and craft of cinematography. Whether you're an aspiring filmmaker, a seasoned professional, or simply a lover of film, these pages promise to illuminate the magic and mechanics of this captivating medium.

The Ever-Changing Canvas of Cinematography

Cinematography, the soul and visual heartbeat of cinema, is an ever-changing landscape, adapting and transforming with technological advancements and creative ingenuity. It's more than simply capturing moving images; it's about painting emotion, story, and aesthetics onto the filmic canvas.

Early Beginnings to Sound and Color

From the artful expressions of the silent era, as seen in "Metropolis," the medium has continually evolved. The introduction of sound with "The Jazz Singer" revolutionized storytelling, and the vibrant transformation with color, as witnessed in "The Wizard of Oz," brought a new layer of depth to the cinematic experience.

Classical Hollywood Cinema: A Golden Age

The classical Hollywood era was marked by the tight control of the studio system, a time when films like "Casablanca" were produced with unparalleled craftsmanship. This era celebrated the art of black and white in "Citizen Kane" and explored the craft of cinematography in masterpieces like "Sunset Boulevard." Lighting techniques became more refined, with films like "Touch of Evil," and the camera movement and composition reached new heights in epics like "Gone with the Wind."

New Waves and Innovations

The arrival of the New Wave brought fresh perspectives and unconventional methods. European New Wave films like "Breathless" broke the rules, while Hollywood responded with counterculture narratives such as "Easy Rider." Technology continued to evolve with digital innovation in "Avatar" and breathtaking special effects in "Inception."

Art, Craft, and Technology in Modern Cinema

Modern cinematography blends art and technology seamlessly, emphasizing composition in films like "The Grand Budapest Hotel" and lighting mastery in "Blade Runner 2049." The changing landscape has also seen the rise of digital cinematography, aerial photography in "Skyfall," and new modes of storytelling in a multiscreen world with films like "Life of Pi."

Genres, Styles, and Global Perspectives

Different genres and styles have enriched cinema, from the evolution of genre in "Pulp Fiction" to experimental films like "Moonlight." Comedy, romance, and action have their unique cinematographic attributes, captured in "The Grand Budapest Hotel," "La La Land," and "John Wick." The global cinematic landscape has been enriched by eastern perspectives such as "Parasite" and the rise of African and Latin cinema in films like "City of God."

Facing the Future

Cinematography's future landscape is as vast as the imagination. Sustainability, ethics in filmmaking as seen in "The Revenant," virtual reality like "Ready Player One," and remote filming in "The Midnight Sky" point towards a future filled with innovation and artistic exploration.

Conclusion

The ever-changing canvas of cinematography represents a constant dance between technology, creativity, and expression. It's a journey through time, culture, and artistry, reflecting human experience in its countless shades. As we look forward, we can only imagine the visual symphonies yet to be composed on this endless canvas. This book serves as a guide, inspiration, and testament to the vibrant life of cinema, an art form that continues to reinvent itself.

Part I: The Foundations

The Foundations form the bedrock of cinematic history, a mesmerizing exploration of technological marvels and artistic innovations that gave rise to the medium we adore today. From the poetic imagery of the silent era to the revolutionary impact of sound and the mesmerizing infusion of color, this part delves into the milestones that defined the early stages of cinema. Guiding us through films such as "Metropolis," "The Jazz Singer," and "The Wizard of Oz," we journey into an age where every frame was a novel experiment, every sound a melody, and every color a brushstroke on the rich canvas of film history.

The Silent Era - Example: "Metropolis"

In the grand history of cinema, the Silent Era occupies a space of profound innovation and experimentation. The absence of sound created a void that filmmakers sought to fill with striking visuals, complex narratives, and inventive storytelling techniques. One film that stood at the pinnacle of this era's artistic achievements was Fritz Lang's "Metropolis."

Released in 1927, "Metropolis" is considered a trailblazing example of science fiction and a monument in cinematic history. Set in a dystopian future, it presents a world divided into two distinct classes: the elite who live above ground, and the oppressed workers who toil below. The film's imagery and themes were groundbreaking and mirrored the societal concerns of the era, particularly the fear of industrialization and the loss of individuality.

"Metropolis" utilized stunning special effects that were far ahead of its time. The film's massive sets, intricate miniatures, and visual trickery produced awe-inspiring scenes that continue to influence modern-day filmmakers. These effects were not mere eye candy but served to enhance the story, creating a world both fantastical and terrifyingly plausible.

Fritz Lang's vision extended beyond visuals, delving into complex character development and symbolism. Maria, the film's central character, is depicted as both an innocent woman and a sinister robot, a duality that explores themes of humanity, technology, and control. This multifaceted portrayal added depth to the silent characters, allowing them to convey emotion and narrative without words.

The film's score played a significant role in communicating emotion. The orchestration, written by Gottfried Huppertz, was tailored to match the film's rhythm and themes. It added texture to the silent images, helping the audience connect with the characters' feelings and the overarching narrative.

"Metropolis" was also a triumph of editing. Its fast-paced cuts and transitions were innovative for the time, helping to build tension and propel the story forward. The editing techniques demonstrated in "Metropolis" laid the groundwork for future filmmakers and remain a masterclass in visual storytelling.

Despite its brilliance, "Metropolis" faced challenges upon its release. The film was heavily edited by distributors, leading to multiple versions that obscured Lang's original vision. The disjointed edits affected the coherence of the story and contributed to mixed critical reception.

Over the years, various attempts have been made to restore "Metropolis" to its original glory. These restorations have helped preserve the film's legacy and allowed new generations to experience Lang's magnum opus as it was meant to be seen.

Beyond its technical achievements, "Metropolis" resonated with audiences due to its social commentary. The film's depiction of class struggle, worker exploitation, and the potential dangers of unchecked technological progress still strikes a chord today.

The visual motifs in "Metropolis" have become synonymous with the Silent Era and continue to be referenced and replicated in contemporary cinema. From dystopian landscapes to the iconic robot Maria, Lang's imagery transcends time.

In academic circles, "Metropolis" is often studied for its combination of German Expressionism and allegorical storytelling. Its influence extends to literature, theater, and visual arts, making it a multidisciplinary masterpiece.

Fritz Lang's dedication to his craft and his refusal to be constrained by the limitations of the time have positioned "Metropolis" as a timeless classic. His efforts to push boundaries inspired subsequent generations of directors, writers, and visual artists.

The legacy of "Metropolis" is not confined to its artistic and technical achievements. It serves as a reminder of cinema's power to reflect society's hopes, fears, and aspirations. It is a mirror held up to the time it was made, yet its reflections resonate in our present day.

The Silent Era is often seen through the lens of limitations, a time before sound added depth to cinematic expression.

However, films like "Metropolis" exemplify how these limitations spurred creativity and innovation.

In conclusion, "Metropolis" is more than just a film; it's a testament to human imagination and the unyielding pursuit of artistic expression. As an emblematic piece of the Silent Era, it continues to inspire, challenge, and captivate audiences, solidifying its place as one of the most significant films in cinematic history.

The Introduction of Sound - Example: "The Jazz Singer"

The history of cinema took a seismic shift with the advent of sound, forever transforming the way audiences experience film. At the heart of this revolution was "The Jazz Singer," the first feature-length motion picture with synchronized dialogue and music, marking the birth of the "talkies."

Released in 1927, "The Jazz Singer" is directed by Alan Crosland and stars Al Jolson as Jakie Rabinowitz, a young man who rebels against his Jewish heritage to pursue a career in jazz singing. Though the film contained limited synchronized dialogue, its blend of Vitaphone sound-on-disc technology with visual imagery made it a historic milestone.

The introduction of sound brought a sense of realism and immersion that was previously unattainable. Audiences were enthralled by the experience of hearing an actor's voice, singing, and the accompanying music, all of which made the film come alive in a new and exciting way.

"The Jazz Singer" faced significant technical challenges during its production. The process of synchronizing sound with visuals was still in its infancy, and even minor discrepancies could create an unsettling effect. The film's success in this area set the standard for others to follow and proved that sound was more than a novelty.

The impact of sound extended beyond the sensory experience; it necessitated a complete overhaul of filmmaking techniques. Directors, actors, and writers had to adapt to this new dimension, rethinking the way scenes were staged, dialogue was delivered, and stories were told.

Sound opened doors for new genres, particularly musicals, which thrived in this new era. "The Jazz Singer" itself, with its memorable musical performances, played a vital role in popularizing this genre, setting the stage for a golden age of musical cinema.

However, the transition was not without its casualties. Many silent film stars found it challenging to adapt to the talkies, either because of their voices or their inability to adjust to the new acting style. Careers were made and broken in this transitional period.

The cultural significance of "The Jazz Singer" extends to its themes and narrative. The story of assimilation, identity, and generational conflict resonated with a society grappling with modernity and change. It provided a glimpse into the tension between tradition and progress, a theme that continues to be relevant.

Economically, the success of "The Jazz Singer" signaled to studios and investors that sound was the future. It led to a rapid investment in sound technology and the retrofitting of theaters, driving the industry towards modernization.

The critical reception of "The Jazz Singer" was mixed, with praise for its technological achievements but criticism for some of its racial representations. The film's use of blackface, a common practice at the time, has led to contemporary debates about its legacy and place in film history.

"The Jazz Singer" was instrumental in shaping the careers of composers, musicians, and singers, providing them with new opportunities to reach audiences. The integration of popular music into film created a symbiotic relationship between these two entertainment forms.

Despite being a product of its time, "The Jazz Singer" has endured as a symbol of innovation. It stands as a testament to human creativity and the relentless pursuit of artistic advancement. Its influence can be seen in the myriad ways sound is used in contemporary cinema, from immersive soundscapes to intricate sound design.

The introduction of sound was not merely a technological shift; it altered the very language of cinema. It added depth, texture, and complexity, allowing filmmakers to explore emotions and themes with a subtlety and nuance that silent films could not achieve.

In the broader context of cultural history, "The Jazz Singer" marks a moment where technology and art converged to redefine entertainment. It captures a time of transformation, mirroring the broader societal shifts of the Roaring Twenties.

In conclusion, "The Jazz Singer" is more than a film; it is a pivotal moment in cinematic history. Its blend of sound and vision ushered in a new era, forever changing the way we watch, hear, and feel movies. Its legacy continues to resonate, reminding us of the power of innovation and the timeless magic of cinema.

Color and Cinematic Expression - Example: "The Wizard of Oz"

If sound transformed the way audiences heard films, color redefined the way they saw them. The 1939 classic "The Wizard of Oz" stands as a seminal example of how color can be an expressive storytelling tool. Its innovative use of Technicolor marked a significant advancement in the art of filmmaking.

Directed by Victor Fleming, "The Wizard of Oz" tells the story of a young girl named Dorothy, transported to a magical world. The film's use of color is no mere technical achievement; it serves as a narrative device, symbolizing themes and emotions within the story.

The movie's transition from sepia-toned Kansas to the vibrantly colored Land of Oz is one of the most iconic moments in cinematic history. This shift not only delighted audiences with its visual splendor but also conveyed a deeper sense of wonder and transformation.

Technicolor was a complex and costly process, requiring specialized cameras, lighting, and processing. "The Wizard of Oz" was one of the first major films to fully embrace this technology, paving the way for a future filled with vivid and captivating color cinema.

Color also played a crucial role in character and set design. The ruby red slippers, the Emerald City, and the contrasting hues of the different lands within Oz became integral to the storytelling, reinforcing the characters' personalities and the fantastical nature of the world.

The film's strategic use of color extended to costuming, makeup, and special effects. Color palettes were carefully chosen to evoke specific emotions, create visual harmony, or add dramatic emphasis, as seen in the distinction between the Wicked Witch's green appearance and Glinda's ethereal glow.

Beyond aesthetics, color in "The Wizard of Oz" serves a symbolic function. The contrast between the drab reality of Kansas and the enchanting world of Oz mirrors the duality of fantasy and reality, childhood innocence and adult wisdom, home, and adventure.

The decision to use color creatively required significant collaboration between the filmmakers, including art directors, costume designers, makeup artists, and cinematographers. This team effort led to a cohesive and immersive visual experience.

The cultural impact of "The Wizard of Oz" extended beyond its release. Its annual broadcasts on television introduced new generations to the magic of color cinema, solidifying its place in the hearts and minds of viewers worldwide.

Though renowned for its visual style, "The Wizard of Oz" also contributed to cinematic storytelling techniques. Its seamless blend of music, special effects, and character development created an engaging and unified narrative experience.

"The Wizard of Oz" spurred further experimentation with color in film, encouraging filmmakers to explore how hues could shape mood, tone, and theme. It set the stage for the artistic use of color that would become integral to modern filmmaking.

The film's achievements in color did not go unrecognized. It won the Academy Award for Best Original Song and Best Original Score and received a special award for its groundbreaking use of Technicolor. Its critical acclaim underscored the power of color as an artistic medium.

The legacy of "The Wizard of Oz" continues to influence contemporary filmmakers, who look to its innovative use of color for inspiration. Its masterful blending of technical prowess and creative vision remains a standard for visual storytelling.

Despite the passage of time, "The Wizard of Oz" continues to enchant audiences. Its use of color transcends mere spectacle, reaching into the realm of art, where color becomes an essential part of the narrative, character, and emotion.

In conclusion, "The Wizard of Oz" symbolizes a pivotal moment in film history where color moved from being a technical novelty to a nuanced and expressive component of cinematic language. Its lasting impact serves as a reminder that technological innovation, when applied with artistry and insight, can create timeless works of art.

Part II: Classical Hollywood Cinema

The Golden Age of Hollywood represents a time when cinema flourished through formal techniques, stringent guidelines, and an assembly-line approach to filmmaking. Classical Hollywood Cinema defined an era marked by the dominance of the studio system, the emergence of definitive genres, and a focus on narrative continuity. In this part, we will explore the intricate studio dynamics in films like "Casablanca," the timeless art of black and white as showcased in "Citizen Kane," and the craft of cinematography that reached its zenith in masterpieces like "Sunset Boulevard." The brilliance of lighting techniques, camera movement, and composition during this period laid down principles that continue to influence modern cinema.

The Studio System - Example: "Casablanca"

The Golden Age and the Studio System:

During the Golden Age of Hollywood, the studio system was the heart of film production. With a handful of studios wielding enormous power, they maintained control over all aspects of filmmaking, including the production, distribution, and exhibition of films. The vertically integrated system allowed the studios to contract actors, writers, directors, and producers, effectively shaping the artistic vision of Hollywood.

"Casablanca" as a Product of the System:

"Casablanca," directed by Michael Curtiz and released in 1942, stands as a quintessential product of the studio system. Produced by Warner Bros., the film is a perfect example of how the studio managed talent, scripts, and production values to create a timeless classic.

Development and Pre-production:

The development of "Casablanca" was representative of the studio-driven approach. From the adaptation of the play "Everybody Comes to Rick's" to the final script, the influence of producers, executives, and studio-hired writers was evident, creating a coherent narrative that matched the studio's vision.

Star Power and Contractual Obligations:

In casting Humphrey Bogart and Ingrid Bergman, Warner Bros. leveraged its contract stars, emphasizing the role of studios in building and controlling the star image. The synergy between the on-screen personas and the roles they played added a unique authenticity to the film.

Directorial Choices:

Curtiz's direction in "Casablanca" is a testament to the craftsmanship encouraged by the studio system. His work, tightly aligned with the studio's requirements, shaped the film's iconic romantic tension, political undertones, and visual aesthetics.

Music and Cinematography:

The film's memorable score, composed by Max Steiner, was an integral part of Warner Bros.' production strategy. The music, combined with Arthur Edeson's cinematography, created an atmospheric experience that brought the exotic setting of Casablanca to life.

Themes and Cultural Relevance:

The themes of love, sacrifice, and wartime patriotism resonated with the wartime audience. Warner Bros. astutely tapped into the zeitgeist, using "Casablanca" as a propaganda tool to promote anti-Nazi sentiment.

Post-production and Release Strategy:

The studio-controlled post-production and release strategy enabled "Casablanca" to have a timely premiere, coinciding with the Allied invasion of North Africa. This alignment further bolstered the film's impact and success.

Awards and Legacy:

Winning three Academy Awards, including Best Picture, "Casablanca" stands as a testament to the efficiency and excellence of the studio system. Its legacy continues to be celebrated as one of the greatest films ever made.

The Studio System's Decline:

By the 1950s, the decline of the studio system had begun, challenged by legal regulations and the rise of television. Yet, the impact of this era, exemplified by "Casablanca," continues to influence the cinematic landscape.

Reflection on the Creative Process:

The tightly controlled creative process in "Casablanca" is both praised for its result and critiqued for its restrictions on artistic freedom. It's a reflection of the constant tension between commerce and artistry within the studio environment.

"Casablanca" as an Educational Tool:

As a case study, "Casablanca" offers valuable insights into classical filmmaking techniques, narrative construction, and the socio-political context of the time. It serves as an essential reference for filmmakers and scholars alike.

Adaptations and Cultural Impact:

The story and characters of "Casablanca" have permeated popular culture, leading to various adaptations and references in films, television, and literature. Its dialogue and scenes are part of the global cinematic lexicon.

The Enduring Appeal:

The magic of "Casablanca" endures, transcending time and generational divides. It continues to captivate audiences, reinforcing the film's status as a timeless product of the studio era.

"Casablanca" serves as a comprehensive illustration of the studio system at its peak. Through the prism of this film, we can explore the intricate relationships between studios, talent, production techniques, and societal influences that shaped an entire era of filmmaking. It's not just a film, but a lesson in cinema history, reflecting the complexity and genius of Hollywood's Golden Age.

The Art of Black and White - Example: "Citizen Kane"

Introduction to Black and White Cinematography:

Black and white cinematography holds a special place in the world of film. It's a medium that speaks in contrasts, textures, and gradients, creating visual poetry that resonates with viewers. "Citizen Kane," directed by Orson Welles, is a prime example of the potential and beauty of this art form.

The Aesthetics of "Citizen Kane":

The striking visual style of "Citizen Kane" was a collaborative effort between Welles and cinematographer Gregg Toland. Together they pushed the boundaries of black and white filmmaking, utilizing deep focus, low-angle shots, and inventive lighting to enhance the story's thematic depth.

Deep Focus Technique:

The deep focus technique used in "Citizen Kane" allowed for extreme depth of field, keeping both the foreground and background sharp. This choice made scenes visually intricate and thematically rich, as it encapsulated different layers of meaning within a single frame.

Low-angle Shots and Expressionism:

Welles' use of low-angle shots made characters appear dominant and imposing. This technique drew from German Expressionism and added a psychological dimension to the characters, especially in the portrayal of Charles Foster Kane.

Chiaroscuro Lighting:

The use of chiaroscuro lighting in "Citizen Kane" created a dramatic contrast between light and shadow. This approach highlighted the internal conflict of characters and underscored the film's motifs of power, mystery, and isolation.

Narrative Structure:

"Citizen Kane" is renowned for its nonlinear narrative structure. The story unfolds through flashbacks and varying perspectives, a method that resonates perfectly with the film's black and white visual treatment, reflecting the complexity and ambiguity of memory and perception.

Symbolism and Visual Metaphors:

The film's black and white imagery is laden with symbols and visual metaphors that deepen the narrative. From the foreboding Xanadu to the iconic snow globe, the visuals echo the film's themes of ambition, loss, and the elusiveness of truth.

Innovation in Set Design and Composition:

The film's set design, along with its compositional choices, broke away from traditional Hollywood norms. The blending of real sets with matte paintings, miniatures, and optical effects created a unique and evocative visual experience.

Sound and Music Integration:

The auditory aspect of "Citizen Kane" complements its visuals. Bernard Herrmann's score, along with innovative sound editing, adds to the film's atmospheric and emotional depth, making the black and white images come alive with added resonance.

Influence on Future Filmmakers:

"Citizen Kane" has left an indelible mark on cinema, influencing generations of filmmakers. Its creative use of black and white cinematography continues to inspire directors seeking to explore the aesthetic and emotional possibilities of this medium.

Critical Reception and Legacy:

Upon its release, "Citizen Kane" received critical acclaim for its technical achievements and narrative innovations. Its enduring status as one of the greatest films ever made testifies to its artistic brilliance and its mastery of black and white cinematography.

Relevance in Modern Cinema:

The aesthetics of "Citizen Kane" find echoes in modern cinema, where black and white is often employed for artistic expression, nostalgia, or thematic emphasis. The film remains a benchmark for those exploring the expressive range of monochromatic visuals.

Educational Value:

For film students and enthusiasts, "Citizen Kane" serves as an essential study in visual storytelling. Its artistic choices and technical innovations provide invaluable insights into the craft of filmmaking.

Cultural Impact and Iconography:

Beyond its cinematic achievements, "Citizen Kane" has become a cultural icon. Its quotes, scenes, and visual style are part of the collective cultural memory, reflecting the film's universal appeal and significance.

"Citizen Kane" is not just a film but an artistic statement that celebrates the myriad possibilities of black and white cinematography. Its combination of innovative techniques, thematic depth, and visual poetry makes it an everlasting testament to the power of monochrome in conveying complex human emotions and narratives. It's a film that invites viewers to explore, analyze, and marvel at the richness of cinema's visual language.

The Craft of Cinematography in the Golden Age - Example: "Sunset Boulevard"

Introduction to "Sunset Boulevard":

Released in 1950, "Sunset Boulevard" is a classic film that stands as a defining work in the Golden Age of Hollywood. Directed by Billy Wilder and featuring cinematography by John F. Seitz, this film-noir is celebrated for its visual storytelling, symbolism, and portrayal of Hollywood's darker side.

Visual Style and Film Noir:

"Sunset Boulevard" epitomizes film-noir with its moody lighting, sharp contrasts, and unsettling angles. The cinematography captures a world that is both glamorous and grim, mirroring the dichotomy of fame and failure in Hollywood.

Use of Lighting:

The lighting in "Sunset Boulevard" is masterful in creating atmosphere and defining character. Shadows and filtered light are used to create a sense of foreboding and to accentuate the psychological complexity of the characters, particularly the faded silent-film star Norma Desmond.

Innovative Camera Angles and Framing:

The film's innovative camera angles and framing techniques contribute to its unique visual language. From the opening shot filmed from inside a swimming pool to the expressive close-ups of Desmond, every choice serves the story and adds to the film's visual allure.

Setting and Production Design:

The lavish set of Desmond's mansion, designed with a blend of opulence and decay, serves as a metaphor for the character's state of mind. The cinematography captures this setting in rich detail, using it to enhance the narrative's themes of obsession and despair.

Iconic Imagery and Symbolism:

"Sunset Boulevard" is filled with iconic imagery and symbols, from the haunting eyes of Desmond's portraits to the winding road of Sunset Boulevard itself. These elements are captured with precision and artistry, adding layers of meaning to the visual narrative.

Narrative Structure and Point of View:

The film's narrative structure is unconventional, with a deceased protagonist narrating the story. The cinematography plays a crucial role in maintaining this point of view, keeping the audience immersed in the unfolding drama.

Performance and Cinematography Integration:

Gloria Swanson's powerful performance as Desmond is amplified by the cinematography. The camera's treatment of her character, through expressive close-ups and dramatic lighting, accentuates her descent into madness and desperation.

Influence of Silent Films:

"Sunset Boulevard" pays homage to the silent film era, incorporating stylistic elements reminiscent of silent cinema. The inclusion of silent-film techniques and references adds a historical dimension and a meta-narrative to the film.

Sound and Music:

The integration of Franz Waxman's haunting score with the film's visuals creates a perfect symbiosis that enhances the mood. Sound and music in "Sunset Boulevard" are meticulously aligned with the cinematography to create a unified and compelling experience.

Cultural Commentary:

Beyond its technical achievements, "Sunset Boulevard" offers a scathing commentary on Hollywood's treatment of its stars and the ruthlessness of the industry. The cinematography plays a crucial role in conveying this critical perspective.

Critical Reception and Legacy:

The cinematography of "Sunset Boulevard" was lauded upon its release and continues to be studied for its innovation and artistry. The film's visual style has influenced countless filmmakers and remains a standout example of cinematography in the Golden Age.

Relevance to Contemporary Cinema:

"Sunset Boulevard" remains relevant to contemporary filmmakers exploring neo-noir or seeking inspiration in its visual storytelling. Its innovative techniques and thematic richness continue to resonate in modern cinematic discourse.

Educational Value for Filmmakers:

For aspiring filmmakers and cinematographers, "Sunset Boulevard" offers a masterclass in visual storytelling. Its successful integration of all cinematographic elements serves as an exemplary model of the craft.

"Sunset Boulevard" stands as a monument to the Golden Age's craft of cinematography. Its blend of stylistic innovation, thematic depth, and visual eloquence makes it a timeless classic. The film continues to inspire, challenge, and mesmerize audiences, affirming its place in the annals of cinematic history. It is a reminder of the power of visuals to tell stories, evoke emotions, and critique society. In the world of cinema, it remains a boulevard that many continue to traverse, finding new insights and inspirations along the way.

Lighting Techniques of Classical Hollywood - Example: "Touch of Evil"

Introduction to "Touch of Evil":

Orson Welles' 1958 film, "Touch of Evil," is a seminal work in the history of cinema, celebrated for its groundbreaking lighting techniques. It serves as a defining example of how lighting can be used to create atmosphere, define characters, and serve the narrative in classical Hollywood filmmaking.

The Opening Shot:

The film's famous opening shot, a three-minute-long unbroken take, is a masterful combination of movement, timing, and lighting. It sets the tone for the film and introduces the viewer to the murky world where the story unfolds.

Low-Key Lighting and Contrast:

"Touch of Evil" employs low-key lighting to create dramatic contrasts and shadows. This approach enhances the film's dark, moody atmosphere and gives depth to the characters and their morally ambiguous world.

Expressionism Influence:

The lighting techniques in the film are heavily influenced by German Expressionism, using exaggerated and stylized lighting to reflect the psychological states of the characters, especially the corrupt police captain, Hank Quinlan.

The Use of Shadows:

Welles makes innovative use of shadows to create tension and reveal character. The shadows often operate as visual metaphors for the hidden and corrupt nature of the characters, enhancing the film's thematic complexity.

Integration with Set Design:

The film's lighting is intricately integrated with its set design. The dark alleys, dimly lit rooms, and seedy bars are all enhanced by the strategic use of lighting, creating an immersive environment that serves the narrative.

Character Definition through Lighting:

Lighting in "Touch of Evil" is used not just to create mood but to define characters. The lighting on Quinlan, played by Welles himself, is particularly noteworthy, reflecting his complex and dark nature.

Innovation in Night Shooting:

"Touch of Evil" was innovative in its approach to night shooting. The film's cinematographer, Russell Metty, worked with Welles to create realistic yet stylized night scenes that are integral to the film's visual identity.

Collaboration between Director and Cinematographer:

Welles' collaboration with Metty is a shining example of the synergy between a director and cinematographer. Their shared vision and attention to detail resulted in a visually cohesive and innovative film.

Naturalistic Approach:

Despite its stylization, "Touch of Evil" employs a naturalistic approach to lighting. The film avoids overly theatrical effects, aiming instead for a gritty realism that adds to the film's authenticity.

Impact on Film Noir:

"Touch of Evil" had a lasting impact on the film noir genre. Its innovative use of lighting went on to influence numerous filmmakers, solidifying its place in the pantheon of visually influential films.

Chiaroscuro Technique:

The film utilizes the chiaroscuro technique, a method of using strong contrasts between light and dark to give volume in modeling three-dimensional objects and figures. This approach lends a painterly quality to the film's visuals.

Cultural Impact and Reception:

The lighting techniques employed in "Touch of Evil" contributed to its critical success and enduring cultural impact. The film continues to be studied for its visual mastery and has inspired generations of filmmakers.

Teaching and Educational Value:

"Touch of Evil" offers invaluable lessons for filmmakers and students in the effective use of lighting. Its combination of artistic vision, technical skill, and storytelling prowess serves as an inspiration and a guide.

"Touch of Evil" stands as a landmark in the history of cinematography, particularly in the realm of lighting. The film's lighting techniques are not merely technical achievements but integral components of the storytelling process. From the opening shot to the final frame, the lighting in "Touch of Evil" serves as a dynamic narrative force, enhancing every aspect of the film. It remains a shining example of how lighting can be harnessed creatively to produce a cinematic masterpiece, reflecting the very essence of classical Hollywood's craft and artistry.

Camera Movement and Composition - Example: "Gone with the Wind"

Introduction to "Gone with the Wind":

Released in 1939 and directed by Victor Fleming, "Gone with the Wind" is hailed as a masterpiece of storytelling and visual composition. Its innovative use of camera movement and framing continues to be a benchmark for cinematographers.

Epic Scope and Grandeur:

The film's epic scale required innovative techniques to capture its grandeur. The sweeping camera movements and panoramic vistas provided audiences with a sense of the vast landscape and societal upheaval of the Civil War era.

Iconic Crane Shots:

The film employed crane shots to breathtaking effect, most famously in the scene showing the wounded in Atlanta. This technique allowed for a bird's-eye view of the chaos, emphasizing the tragedy of war.

Character-Centric Composition:

The composition within scenes often centered characters, such as Scarlett O'Hara, within the frame to reflect their emotions and perspectives. This character-driven approach to framing added depth to the performances and connected the audience to the protagonists.

Use of Dolly Shots:

Dolly shots were used to follow characters, enhancing the film's emotional resonance. One such moment occurs during Scarlett's determined walk through the plantation fields, allowing the audience to feel her resolve.

Innovation in Color:

"Gone with the Wind" was one of the early films to embrace Technicolor, and it used color to accentuate mood and emotion. The burning of Atlanta, with its vibrant reds and oranges, remains an unforgettable visual moment.

Depth of Field:

The film made excellent use of deep focus, allowing multiple planes within a scene to be in focus simultaneously. This technique enriched the visual texture and complexity of the film.

Blocking and Choreography:

The careful choreography of actors and the camera allowed for dynamic scenes that flowed naturally. This was essential in scenes with large ensembles, where precise blocking and camera movement were coordinated seamlessly.

Symbolic Composition:

The film often employed symbolism within its composition, using visual cues to reinforce themes and character arcs. For example, the framing of characters against windows and doors often signified changes or decisions in their lives.

Transition Techniques:

"Gone with the Wind" utilized innovative transitions, such as dissolves and wipes, to guide the audience through the sprawling narrative. These transitions contributed to the film's fluid storytelling.

Integration with Set Design and Lighting:

The composition and camera movement were closely integrated with set design and lighting, creating a visual harmony. This synergy provided a rich and immersive visual experience.

Influence on Future Filmmakers:

The techniques used in "Gone with the Wind" had a profound impact on future filmmakers. Its innovations in camera movement and composition became reference points for generations to come.

Legacy and Preservation:

The film's visual legacy has been preserved and celebrated over the years. Its restoration efforts have ensured that future audiences can experience it in its full visual splendor.

Conclusion of the Overall Style of Classical Hollywood Cinematography:

"Gone with the Wind" epitomizes the style and technical excellence of classical Hollywood cinematography. Its use of camera movement and composition not only served the story but also elevated the entire cinematic experience. The film's commitment to visual storytelling remains a testament to the power of cinema.

"Gone with the Wind" stands as a monumental achievement in the history of film. Its innovative and artful use of camera movement and composition continues to inspire and educate filmmakers. The film's visual language transcends its era, solidifying its place as a timeless classic that showcases the potential of camera work to capture the human experience in all its complexity and grandeur. It serves as a lasting reminder of the craftsmanship that defined the golden age of Hollywood and continues to influence modern cinema.

Conclusion of the overall style of Classical Hollywood Cinematography

The style of Classical Hollywood Cinematography, which emerged during the golden age of cinema, represents an era when storytelling was at the heart of filmmaking. A cohesive and sophisticated visual language was developed during this time, one that prioritized narrative clarity and emotional resonance. With a strong emphasis on continuity, the classical style created seamless transitions between scenes, guiding the audience effortlessly through the storyline.

One of the defining characteristics of this period was the mastery of lighting. Directors of photography like Gregg Toland worked in close collaboration with directors to sculpt light and shadow, creating depth and mood. This lighting technique became instrumental in conveying character emotions and inner thoughts, adding a layer of complexity to the storytelling.

The use of framing and composition was equally integral to the style. Compositional rules were established to guide the eye, focusing the viewer's attention on significant details and characters. Whether it was through the innovative use of deep focus or careful positioning of elements within the frame, filmmakers utilized visual cues to support the narrative.

Camera movement also played a vital role in the style of classical Hollywood cinematography. From the sweeping crane shots to intimate dolly movements, camera techniques were deployed to reflect the emotional state of characters or to give the audience a sense of space and time. These movements were executed with precision, keeping the audience immersed in the world of the film.

A focus on genre also defined this era, with filmmakers employing specific visual motifs to establish the mood of different genres. Whether it was the dark shadows of film noir or the bright and optimistic framing of musicals, cinematographers used their craft to support the thematic elements of various genres, enriching the film's impact.

The collaboration between different departments was at its peak during this period, with art direction, set design, and costuming working hand-in-hand with cinematography. This interdepartmental synergy created a unified visual experience, where every aspect of the film's visuals served the story.

Furthermore, classical Hollywood cinematography embraced technological advancements of its time, such as the introduction of color. Filmmakers like Victor Fleming harnessed color to enhance storytelling, using hues to evoke emotions and highlight significant narrative elements.

Despite the advent of new technologies and shifting trends, the core principles of classical Hollywood cinematography continue to influence modern filmmaking. The attention to narrative clarity, character-driven storytelling, and the elegant use of visual tools remains relevant in contemporary cinema.

In conclusion, the style of Classical Hollywood Cinematography laid the groundwork for the visual language of cinema. By developing techniques and principles that prioritize storytelling and emotional connection, this era has left an indelible mark on the art of filmmaking. Its legacy continues to inspire and guide filmmakers, proving that the artistic choices and technological innovations of the past can resonate across generations and contribute to the evolution of the medium.

Part III: The New Wave

As we journey beyond the cohesive boundaries of classical Hollywood cinema, we find ourselves immersed in the tumultuous and revolutionary waves of the New Wave cinema. With the emergence of audacious filmmakers and avant-garde techniques, the 1960s marked a significant departure from the traditional norms of filmmaking. In this part, we will explore the European New Wave, marked by iconoclastic works such as "Breathless," and then venture into Hollywood's response, epitomized by films like "Easy Rider." The chapters within this part will unveil how this era challenged conventional storytelling, experimenting with narrative structures, visual styles, and thematic depth, forever altering the course of cinematic expression.

European New Wave - Example: "Breathless"

Introduction to the European New Wave: The European New Wave, a movement that originated in the late 1950s and early 1960s, reshaped the world of cinema with its radical techniques, bold storytelling, and defiance of traditional conventions. Within this wave, Jean-Luc Godard's "Breathless" stands as an epitome of what cinema could be when liberated from its conventional shackles.

"Breathless" - A New Approach to Storytelling: "Breathless" is a French film released in 1960, a narrative that doesn't follow a linear path but instead focuses on moments, impressions, and the existential angst of its characters. This approach marked a significant departure from the prevailing storytelling techniques of the time.

The Use of Jump Cuts: One of the defining features of "Breathless" was its pioneering use of jump cuts. This method disrupted the flow of scenes and created a unique visual rhythm, reflecting the chaotic inner life of its protagonists and serving as a visual metaphor for the societal unrest of the time.

The Influence of Jazz: The film's jazz-infused score encapsulates its improvisational spirit. Godard allowed the characters to roam freely within scenes, capturing their dialogues and movements in a way that mirrored a jazz composition, free and unscripted.

Challenging Gender Norms: The female lead, Patricia, played by Jean Seberg, challenged the traditional depictions of women in cinema. Her complex and independent character stood in contrast to the passive roles women were often confined to, reflecting a shift in societal perspectives on gender.

Authenticity and Realism: "Breathless" abandoned the polished look of studio productions, opting instead for on-location shooting and natural lighting. This lent a raw and authentic feel to the film, grounding it in a reality that audiences could connect with.

Embracing Controversy: The film's themes of amorality, existential despair, and defiance of authority were highly controversial for the time. "Breathless" did not shy away from these issues but embraced them, opening the door for future films to explore complex and contentious subjects.

Impact on Cinematography: The cinematographic techniques used in "Breathless" were revolutionary, influencing filmmakers around the world. The handheld camera work, the lack of artificial lighting, and the willingness to break visual continuity set a new standard for cinematic expression.

An Unconventional Love Story: At its heart, "Breathless" is a love story, but one that defies the clichés of romance. The relationship between the characters is fraught with ambiguity and detachment, reflecting a disillusionment with traditional romantic ideals.

Intertextual References: Godard filled "Breathless" with references to other works of art, including literature, painting, and cinema. These intertextual links create a rich tapestry that places the film within a broader cultural context.

The Influence on Future Filmmakers: "Breathless" has had a profound impact on filmmakers across generations. Its aesthetic and thematic innovations continue to inspire directors, making it a timeless piece of cinema that transcends its era.

Reflection of the Times: The film's rebellious spirit was emblematic of the youth culture and political climate of the late 1950s and early 1960s. It resonated with a generation that was questioning societal norms and seeking to redefine itself.

A Commercial Success: Despite its unconventional approach, "Breathless" achieved commercial success, proving that audiences were ready for a new kind of cinema. It marked a turning point, demonstrating that art and commercial success were not mutually exclusive.

The Legacy of "Breathless": More than six decades after its release, "Breathless" continues to be studied, admired, and celebrated. Its boldness and innovation have ensured its place in the pantheon of great films, and it remains a touchstone for anyone seeking to understand the evolution of modern cinema.

Conclusion: "Breathless" is more than just a film; it is a statement, a challenge, and an enduring work of art. It not only defined the European New Wave but also changed the landscape of cinema forever. By breaking free from conventional storytelling and embracing a new form of cinematic language, it paved the way for countless filmmakers to explore, innovate, and redefine the boundaries of what cinema could be. The significance of "Breathless" is not merely historical; it is a living testament to the transformative power of art.

Hollywood's Response - Example: "Easy Rider"

Introduction to "Easy Rider": Released in 1969, "Easy Rider" was a direct response to the European New Wave, bringing its innovative spirit to Hollywood. This film, directed by Dennis Hopper, became a symbol of rebellion, freedom, and a new direction for American cinema.

The Story and Its Reflection of a Generation: "Easy Rider" follows two bikers on a journey across the American landscape, exploring themes of freedom, counterculture, and disillusionment. The narrative encapsulated the sentiments of a generation questioning traditional American values during a time of great societal change.

Innovative Cinematography: The film's use of real locations, natural lighting, and unconventional camera techniques borrowed from the European New Wave. It embraced a raw, gritty aesthetic that broke away from the polished look of mainstream Hollywood productions.

The Soundtrack - A Cultural Statement: The soundtrack of "Easy Rider" featured contemporary rock music from artists like The Byrds, Jimi Hendrix, and Steppenwolf. The use of popular music in place of a traditional score added an authentic voice to the film and helped define it as a cultural icon.

Challenging the Studio System: Produced on a low budget, "Easy Rider" challenged the dominance of the studio system, proving that successful films could be made outside the conventional Hollywood structure. Its commercial success paved the way for more independent filmmaking.

Depiction of Subcultures: Through its portrayal of hippies, drug use, and communal living, "Easy Rider" presented a view of subcultures often ignored or stereotyped by mainstream cinema. It gave voice to alternative lifestyles, reflecting the complexity and diversity of American society.

The Impact on Acting and Casting: By casting Peter Fonda, Dennis Hopper, and Jack Nicholson, who were not typical leading men of the time, "Easy Rider" challenged conventional casting norms. Their authentic performances added depth and realism to the characters, influencing future casting decisions in Hollywood.

Political Commentary: Amidst the Vietnam War and civil rights movement, "Easy Rider" provided political commentary, critiquing government, societal constraints, and the loss of the American dream. Its political undertones resonated with audiences, allowing cinema to be seen as a platform for social critique.

Influence on Road Movies: "Easy Rider" helped establish the road movie genre, focusing on the journey rather than the destination. This emphasis on exploration and self-discovery inspired countless films, cementing a new genre within American cinema.

The Editing Style: The film's nonlinear editing, fragmented scenes, and quick cuts were reflective of the disjointed experience of the 1960s youth. The innovative editing contributed to a feeling of dislocation and search for meaning that mirrored the existential questions of the era.

Cult Status and Cultural Impact: "Easy Rider" quickly achieved cult status and became a symbol of a generation. Its impact extended beyond cinema, influencing fashion, music, and the broader cultural landscape.

Opening Doors for New Filmmakers: The success of "Easy Rider" opened doors for new directors and writers who wished to explore unconventional themes. It marked the beginning of the New Hollywood era, where creative control was often handed to filmmakers rather than studios.

A Reflection of America's Social Fabric: By portraying a complex, multifaceted image of America, "Easy Rider" allowed viewers to reflect on their society's contradictions, hopes, and fears. It did not offer simple answers but prompted audiences to think critically about the world around them.

The Legacy of "Easy Rider": Over five decades later, "Easy Rider" continues to be studied and appreciated for its groundbreaking approach to storytelling, cinematography, and cultural commentary. Its influence is still felt in contemporary cinema and stands as a testament to the transformative power of film.

Conclusion: "Easy Rider" was more than just a movie; it was a seismic shift in Hollywood that resonated deeply with audiences and filmmakers alike. By embracing the innovations of the European New Wave and infusing them with an American spirit, it created a new cinematic language.

Its boldness, authenticity, and willingness to challenge norms have ensured its place as one of the defining films of the 20th century, symbolizing a moment when cinema became a medium for social reflection, exploration, and revolution.

Part IV: Technological Transformations

As the reel of film history unravels, the Technological Transformations chapter showcases a breathtaking revolution in the art and craft of cinematography. From the digital wonders that brought fantastical worlds to life to the modern special effects that redefined what's possible on screen, this part dives into the technological advancements that have shaped contemporary cinema. With a focus on examples like "Avatar" and "Inception," it explores how the digital era has allowed filmmakers to break boundaries and create visual spectacles that engage and astonish audiences like never before.

Digital Innovation - Example: "Avatar"

Introduction to "Avatar": The 2009 film "Avatar," directed by James Cameron, marked a significant milestone in the world of digital innovation within the film industry. Utilizing state-of-the-art technology and groundbreaking techniques, the film redefined what was possible in cinematic storytelling, forever altering the landscape of movie-making.

The World of Pandora: The fictional universe of Pandora, where "Avatar" is set, is a visual masterpiece. The creation of this intricate, colorful, and breathtaking world required an unprecedented use of digital technology, with new software being developed to handle the film's unique requirements.

3D Cinematography: "Avatar" took 3D cinematography to new heights. The Fusion Camera System, specifically designed for the film, allowed a level of depth and immersion previously unseen. This technological advancement not only enhanced the visual experience but opened up new narrative possibilities.

Motion Capture Technology: The Na'vi, the indigenous people of Pandora, were brought to life through a revolutionary motion capture system that accurately translated the actors' performances into digital characters. This allowed for emotive, lifelike animations, bridging the gap between human performance and digital creation.

Virtual Production: The blend of live-action with digitally created environments was groundbreaking in "Avatar." Virtual cameras allowed filmmakers to interact with the virtual world in real-time, blending the lines between reality and imagination.

Environmental Themes and Digital Innovation: Thematically, "Avatar" explored environmental conservation and the respect for nature. Ironically, its digital innovation required vast computational resources. The juxtaposition of these themes and the technology used made the film an intriguing case study in modern cinematography.

Sound and Music: The audio landscape in "Avatar" was as revolutionary as the visuals. The creation of alien languages, the blending of natural and artificial sounds, and the thematic music score all contributed to a full sensory immersion.

Impact on the Audience: The immersive experience of "Avatar" left a lasting impression on audiences around the world. Its technological innovations allowed viewers to lose themselves in a fictional world, setting new expectations for cinematic experiences.

Influence on the Industry: The technological advancements in "Avatar" have had a profound impact on the film industry. The tools and techniques developed for the film have become industry standards, influencing numerous productions since its release.

Criticism and Controversy: Despite its technological achievements, "Avatar" faced criticism. Some argued that the narrative relied on stereotypical tropes, and the extensive use of digital technology led to debates about authenticity in cinema.

Awards and Recognitions: "Avatar" received numerous awards and recognitions, including Oscars for Best Art Direction, Best Cinematography, and Best Visual Effects. These accolades further highlighted its groundbreaking contributions to the film industry.

The Financial Aspect: With a production budget of over $230 million, "Avatar" was a significant financial investment. Its success at the box office, becoming one of the highest-grossing films of all time, demonstrated the commercial potential of digital innovation.

Legacy: More than a decade after its release, "Avatar" continues to be a reference point for digital innovation in filmmaking. Its legacy is seen not only in the technological advancements it spurred but also in the new generation of filmmakers inspired by its creative vision.

Future Implications: As we look towards the future, "Avatar" serves as a reminder of the infinite possibilities that digital innovation presents. The lessons learned and the boundaries pushed by this film continue to inspire exploration and experimentation in cinematic storytelling.

Conclusion: "Avatar" was more than a film; it was a monumental achievement in digital innovation. By leveraging technology to create an immersive, visually stunning world, it expanded the horizons of what is possible in cinema. Its impact resonates across the industry, setting a precedent for creativity, innovation, and storytelling in the digital age. The exploration of Pandora marked not just a thrilling cinematic journey but a revolutionary leap in the ever-evolving art of filmmaking.

Modern Special Effects - Example: "Inception"

Introduction to "Inception": Released in 2010, Christopher Nolan's "Inception" is a landmark film that illustrates the power and artistry of modern special effects. Through a combination of cutting-edge technology and innovative storytelling, "Inception" offers a captivating look into the realm of dreams and the subconscious, setting new standards for visual storytelling.

Plot and Concept: Centered around the theme of dreams within dreams, "Inception" required complex special effects to create believable, layered realities. The concept of entering another person's dream world called for visuals that defied conventional physics, and the film's special effects were pivotal in achieving this.

Practical Effects and CGI: Unlike many contemporary films that rely heavily on CGI, "Inception" blended practical effects with computer-generated imagery. The film's iconic rotating hallway scene is a testament to this approach, where a real, physically rotating set was used alongside digital enhancements.

Zero Gravity Scenes: Crafting the illusion of weightlessness was another challenging feat. By employing wirework, rotating sets, and meticulously planned camera movements, the film created convincing zero-gravity experiences, pushing the boundaries of special effects.

The Dream Layers: Each level of the dream had its own physics and visual style. The creation of these layers required an in-depth understanding of visual effects, from the rainy city streets to the weightless hotel corridors, and the snow-capped mountain fortress.

Visual Metaphors and Symbolism: The film used special effects not only for spectacle but also as metaphors and symbols that tied into the plot. Collapsing dreamscapes and fracturing mirrors served as visual representations of the characters' psychological states.

Sound and Music: Hans Zimmer's score, coupled with intricate sound design, worked in tandem with the visual effects to create an immersive sensory experience. The integration of audio and visuals was paramount in conveying the film's complex narrative.

Challenges and Innovations: Achieving the visual complexity of "Inception" was no small feat. From simulating realistic water effects to designing intricate dream architecture, the filmmakers had to innovate and problem-solve at every turn.

Influence on Filmmaking: The techniques and methodologies used in "Inception" have had a lasting impact on the industry, influencing subsequent films. Its blend of practical and digital effects continues to inspire filmmakers to push the envelope.

Awards and Recognition: "Inception" won four Academy Awards, including Best Visual Effects. Its success at the awards affirmed its status as a groundbreaking film in the realm of special effects.

Cultural Impact: Beyond its technical achievements, "Inception" resonated with audiences and became a cultural phenomenon. Its visual style and themes have permeated pop culture, making it a symbol of cinematic innovation.

Criticism and Analysis: While widely praised, "Inception" also faced criticism for its complexity and ambiguity. Some argued that its reliance on special effects overshadowed character development. Nevertheless, it sparked debates and discussions, reflecting its thought-provoking nature.

Budget and Box Office: With a budget of $160 million, "Inception" was a major investment. Its box office success, grossing over $800 million worldwide, demonstrated the commercial potential of films that are both visually stunning and intellectually engaging.

Legacy: A decade later, "Inception" continues to be regarded as a masterpiece of modern cinema. Its approach to special effects, blending artistry with technology, set a precedent that challenges and inspires filmmakers today.

Conclusion: "Inception" is more than just a visually impressive film; it is a testament to the power of imagination, creativity, and technological innovation. By pushing the boundaries of what is possible on screen, it has expanded the language of cinema, leaving an indelible mark on the art of filmmaking. The dreamscape of "Inception" offers a rich canvas for exploring the human psyche, and its technological accomplishments continue to resonate, cementing its place in the pantheon of films that have redefined the cinematic experience.

Part V: The Art and Craft

Cinematography is more than technology and technique; it's an art form that requires mastery and creativity. In Part V: The Art and Craft, we'll delve into the intricate details that transform moving images into compelling narratives. From the subtleties of composition and framing, as seen in films like "The Grand Budapest Hotel," to the evolving landscape of digital cinematography exemplified by "Slumdog Millionaire," this section explores the artistic vision and craftsmanship behind the lens. Here, we'll uncover the skills that enable cinematographers to manipulate light, movement, and perspective to tell stories in visually stunning and emotive ways.

Composition and Framing - Example: "The Grand Budapest Hotel"

Introduction to Composition and Framing: The mastery of composition and framing is a cornerstone in the world of cinematography. "The Grand Budapest Hotel," directed by Wes Anderson, offers a rich illustration of this aspect, demonstrating how the layout of a scene can captivate audiences and elevate storytelling.

Symmetry in Framing: Anderson's famous use of symmetry gives a distinct visual style that pleases the eye. Each shot is meticulously balanced, and objects are often centered within the frame, giving the film a unique, painterly quality that sets it apart from other films.

Use of Color: In "The Grand Budapest Hotel," color is not merely decorative but serves a narrative purpose. The palette changes with different time periods in the film, guiding the audience through temporal shifts and reflecting the emotional tones of each era.

Aspect Ratio Changes: By employing various aspect ratios, Anderson delineates different timelines in the movie. These changes in aspect ratio are not just stylistic choices but guide the audience through different periods, creating a sense of nostalgia and authenticity.

Character Framing: Characters in the film are framed in a way that provides insights into their personality and role. The way they occupy space within the frame contributes to our understanding of their relationships, social standing, and emotions.

Depth and Perspective: Anderson's use of depth in framing layers characters and objects, providing visual interest and driving the viewer's eye to focal points. The hotel itself becomes a character, with its grandiose architecture and intricate details adding dimensionality to the story.

Geometry and Patterns: The use of geometric patterns and strong lines in the composition of scenes in "The Grand Budapest Hotel" enhances visual harmony. This approach conveys a sense of order, reflecting the highly controlled environment within the hotel.

Camera Movement: Although known for static, perfectly composed shots, Anderson also employs deliberate camera movements in this film. These movements emphasize key narrative moments, leading the audience's gaze to important elements within the frame.

Comedic Framing: Comedy is vital in the film, and the framing contributes to the humor. Anderson's precise timing and composition create visual jokes that are as crucial to the comedy as the witty dialogue.

Emotional Impact through Composition: Composition in "The Grand Budapest Hotel" is not just visually appealing; it also carries emotional weight. The film's framed shots can evoke feelings of isolation, joy, or tension, enhancing the emotional resonance with the audience.

Influence on Modern Filmmaking: The artistic choices in "The Grand Budapest Hotel" have inspired a generation of filmmakers. Anderson's unique approach to composition and framing has become influential, contributing to the discourse on visual storytelling techniques.

Challenges and Criticisms: While praised for its artistic vision, some critics argue that the overemphasis on composition in "The Grand Budapest Hotel" can sometimes overshadow character development and narrative depth. The highly stylized approach may not resonate with every viewer.

The Role of Collaboration: Anderson's vision was realized through collaboration with cinematographer Robert Yeoman. Their partnership highlights how composition and framing are often the result of a shared creative process between the director and cinematographer.

Conclusion: "The Grand Budapest Hotel" stands as a testament to the power of composition and framing in film. Its precise and artistic use of these elements not only defines its aesthetic but adds depth to the story, characters, and emotions.

Relevance to Contemporary Cinema: The significance of "The Grand Budapest Hotel" in modern cinema cannot be overstated. It showcases how attention to composition and framing can elevate a film from mere entertainment to a work of art. This film serves as both inspiration and education for aspiring filmmakers and enthusiasts, illustrating how these vital elements of cinematography can be harnessed to create visually stunning and emotionally engaging films.

Mastery of Lighting - Example: "Blade Runner 2049"

Introduction to Mastery of Lighting: The craft of lighting is an essential element of cinematography, and "Blade Runner 2049" stands as an exceptional example of this artistry. Through the thoughtful use of lighting, the film constructs a vivid and immersive world that enhances the narrative and characters.

The Futuristic Aesthetic: Cinematographer Roger Deakins utilized innovative lighting techniques to portray a futuristic, dystopian world. The choices in lighting design helped create a visual atmosphere that is both alluring and unsettling, encapsulating the film's thematic content.

Color Grading: The film's unique color palette, created through meticulous grading, contributes to the story's mood. The cold blues, warm oranges, and artificial neon all serve to set the emotional tone of different scenes.

Natural and Artificial Light Sources: The juxtaposition of natural and artificial light within "Blade Runner 2049" provides a visual commentary on the blurred lines between humanity and artificial intelligence. This lighting concept accentuates the existential questions raised in the film.

Shadow Play: Deakins masterfully employed shadows to add depth and texture to scenes. Shadows were used not merely as aesthetic elements but as tools to emphasize character traits, emotions, and to reinforce the story's underlying themes.

Use of Practical Lights: In many scenes, lighting instruments are visible within the frame, serving both as practical lights and as part of the set design. This decision adds to the realism of the depicted future world, making it tangible and lived-in.

Lighting the Characters: Character lighting in "Blade Runner 2049" is done with precision, enhancing the personality and emotional state of each character. The lighting choices reflect, reinforce, and sometimes even challenge our understanding of the characters and their journey.

Emphasizing Scale: Through lighting, the film emphasizes the grand scale of its dystopian world. Wide shots are illuminated to show the vastness of the landscapes and cityscapes, contributing to the feeling of a sprawling, overwhelming future environment.

Creating Visual Tension: Deakins used lighting to build visual tension in key sequences. Through contrasts, shadows, and color choices, the lighting design aids in developing the suspense and drama that drive the plot.

Challenges and Innovations: Achieving the unique look of "Blade Runner 2049" was not without challenges. The use of innovative technologies, like synchronized LED panels, allowed for unprecedented control over lighting, giving birth to visually stunning scenes.

Environmental Consciousness: The production also took into consideration sustainable practices, using energy-efficient lighting techniques. This approach not only aligns with the film's thematic concerns but also sets an example for modern film productions.

Impact on Contemporary Cinema: The mastery of lighting in "Blade Runner 2049" has left an indelible mark on modern cinematography. It has inspired a renewed interest in the artistic possibilities of lighting and has set a new standard for visual storytelling.

Reception and Awards: The brilliance of the film's lighting did not go unnoticed. Roger Deakins's work on "Blade Runner 2049" earned him an Academy Award for Best Cinematography, recognizing the vital role that lighting played in the film's success.

Conclusion: "Blade Runner 2049" exemplifies the power of lighting in cinema. It demonstrates how innovative and thoughtful lighting can elevate a film to a work of art, enriching the narrative and providing a profound visual experience.

Relevance to Aspiring Filmmakers: The film serves as an invaluable resource for those studying or working in film. Its lighting techniques, ranging from the technical to the symbolic, offer a rich field of exploration and inspiration. The mastery displayed in "Blade Runner 2049" provides a pathway for the next generation of filmmakers to push the boundaries of what can be achieved through the art of lighting.

Digital Cinematography and the Changing Landscape - Example: "Slumdog Millionaire"

Introduction to Digital Cinematography in "Slumdog Millionaire": The film "Slumdog Millionaire" is emblematic of a new era in cinematography. With its blending of digital cameras, on-location shooting, and post-production technology, it represents a significant shift in how films are made and experienced.

A New Aesthetic: Director Danny Boyle and cinematographer Anthony Dod Mantle harnessed digital cinematography to create a raw and vibrant visual style. This aesthetic gave the film an immediacy that was crucial to its emotional impact.

Versatility of Digital Cameras: The use of digital cameras allowed for flexibility and adaptability during shooting. The filmmakers were able to capture Mumbai's bustling streets and crowded slums authentically, providing a rich visual context for the story.

Editing and Visual Effects: Digital technology facilitated seamless integration of visual effects and editing. The film's unique narrative structure, with its jumps between past and present, was enhanced through the use of digital tools.

Color Grading: The film's color grading played a pivotal role in storytelling, with different color schemes being used to distinguish between various time periods and emotional states. Digital grading technology allowed for this nuanced manipulation of color.

Accessibility and Democratization: "Slumdog Millionaire" is an example of how digital technology has opened up opportunities for filmmakers. Reduced costs and increased accessibility have democratized the field, allowing for new voices to emerge.

Cultural Sensitivity and Authenticity: By shooting on location and using digital methods, the filmmakers were able to engage with local culture more deeply. This approach resulted in a film that felt both globally relevant and culturally specific.

The Soundtrack and Sound Design: Alongside visual innovation, the film embraced new audio techniques. The soundtrack and sound design were integral to the storytelling, with digital audio technology playing a key role.

Impact on the Audience: The film's unique blend of digital techniques created an immersive experience. The audience was drawn into the world of the characters in a way that felt fresh and engaging.

Awards and Recognition: "Slumdog Millionaire" received critical acclaim for its innovative approach, winning eight Academy Awards, including Best Cinematography. This was a significant validation of digital cinematography's place in mainstream cinema.

Challenges of Digital Filmmaking: Despite its advantages, digital cinematography also presents challenges. The film's team had to navigate issues related to data storage, color consistency, and on-location shooting with sensitive equipment.

Sustainability and Ethical Considerations: Digital filmmaking has implications for sustainability, particularly in data management and energy consumption. "Slumdog Millionaire" opens up discussions about how to approach filmmaking responsibly in a digital age.

Global Reach and Influence: The film's success had a wide-reaching impact, influencing filmmakers around the world. It demonstrated the potential of digital technology to transcend cultural and geographical boundaries.

Conclusion: "Slumdog Millionaire" is not just a compelling story; it's a testament to the transformative power of digital cinematography. Its innovative approach to visual storytelling redefined what is possible, marking a pivotal moment in the evolution of cinema.

Relevance to Modern Filmmakers: As a case study, "Slumdog Millionaire" offers insights and inspiration to aspiring filmmakers. Its blend of creativity, technology, and cultural awareness provides a blueprint for how to make resonant and visually stunning films in the digital era.

The Rise of Aerial and Drone Photography - Example: "Skyfall"

Introduction to Aerial and Drone Photography in "Skyfall": Aerial and drone photography have revolutionized the world of cinematography, enabling filmmakers to capture shots that were previously unimaginable. "Skyfall," directed by Sam Mendes and cinematographed by Roger Deakins, is a striking example of this technology's potential.

Shifting Perspectives: Aerial shots in "Skyfall" are used to dramatic effect, providing sweeping views of landscapes and cities. These shots emphasize the global scope of the narrative and underscore the film's thematic elements.

Drone Versatility: Drones were utilized in "Skyfall" to achieve complex shots with precision and grace. Their maneuverability allows for sequences that would have been difficult or impossible to achieve with traditional methods.

Seamless Integration: Aerial and drone shots in "Skyfall" are seamlessly integrated into the film's visual language. This creates a coherent and immersive experience that does not detract from the storytelling.

Enhancing Action Sequences: Aerial photography played a significant role in enhancing the film's thrilling action sequences. These shots provide an elevated perspective that adds dynamism and intensity.

Cost-Effectiveness: Using drones can be a more economical option compared to traditional aerial photography methods. This accessibility enables filmmakers to experiment with different angles and movements without overextending budgets.

Safety Considerations: Drone photography offers safer alternatives for capturing aerial views. "Skyfall" demonstrates how risk can be minimized without sacrificing visual impact.

Environmental Concerns: While drones offer new possibilities, they also present environmental considerations. Filmmakers must navigate regulations and ensure that their usage is responsible and respectful of natural landscapes.

Technological Challenges: The use of drones and aerial photography requires specific technological know-how. "Skyfall's" crew leveraged cutting-edge technology to achieve breathtaking results, showcasing the importance of innovation and adaptability.

Influence on Future Filmmaking: "Skyfall" has been influential in showcasing the artistic and storytelling possibilities offered by aerial and drone photography. Its success has paved the way for continued exploration of these techniques.

Symbolism and Metaphor: Beyond the practical applications, aerial shots in "Skyfall" are imbued with symbolism. These soaring views resonate with themes of surveillance, omnipresence, and the character's internal journey.

Ethical Considerations: As with any technology, aerial and drone photography come with ethical implications. Filmmakers must weigh privacy concerns and legal restrictions, carefully considering how and where they deploy these tools.

Aesthetic Choices: The aesthetics of aerial and drone shots in "Skyfall" are deliberate and artfully composed. This demonstrates how these techniques can be more than mere spectacle, contributing to the film's overall visual artistry.

Conclusion: "Skyfall" is a testament to the transformative power of aerial and drone photography in modern cinema. Its innovative use of these technologies offers lessons in creativity, technical mastery, and ethical consideration.

Relevance to Modern Filmmakers: As technology continues to advance, the opportunities for aerial and drone photography will only expand. "Skyfall" serves as a valuable reference point for filmmakers looking to explore these techniques, pushing the boundaries of what is possible in visual storytelling.

Cinematic Storytelling in a Multiscreen World - Example: "Life of Pi"

Introduction to "Life of Pi" and Multiscreen Storytelling: Ang Lee's "Life of Pi" is a groundbreaking film that utilizes multiscreen technologies to create a captivating cinematic experience. This chapter will explore how multiscreen storytelling shaped the film's narrative and aesthetics.

The Concept of Multiscreen Storytelling: Multiscreen storytelling is an innovative approach that uses multiple screens or displays to enhance the viewer's engagement. In

"Life of Pi," this technique is woven into the narrative, adding depth and dimension.

Visual Design and Composition: The film's visual design is a masterpiece of complexity and coherence. Utilizing multiscreen technology, the filmmakers were able to craft scenes that are visually stunning and thematically resonant.

Impact on Audience Engagement: Multiscreen storytelling in "Life of Pi" fosters a unique engagement with the audience. The use of multiple screens allows for a more immersive experience, drawing viewers into the world of the film.

Thematic Resonance: By employing multiscreen storytelling, "Life of Pi" adds layers of meaning to its themes of faith, survival, and storytelling itself. This technology allows the audience to explore these themes from various angles and perspectives.

Innovation in Adaptation: Adapting Yann Martel's novel into a multiscreen experience was a significant creative challenge. Ang Lee's approach offers insights into how innovative technology can enrich literary adaptations.

Collaboration and Integration: "Life of Pi" demonstrates the collaborative effort required to successfully implement multiscreen storytelling. From direction to cinematography to post-production, the integration of this technique required a cohesive vision.

Technical Challenges and Solutions: Implementing multiscreen storytelling in "Life of Pi" posed several technical challenges. The solutions found highlight the importance of technological ingenuity in modern filmmaking.

Accessibility and Usability: While multiscreen technology offers new possibilities, it also raises questions about accessibility and usability for different audiences. "Life of Pi" addressed these considerations with careful design choices.

Multiscreen Storytelling as Artistic Expression: Beyond its technical applications, multiscreen storytelling in "Life of Pi" is an artistic expression. It's used as a tool to expand the film's visual language and deepen its emotional impact.

Cultural Impact: "Life of Pi" has had a lasting impact on the cinematic landscape, inspiring filmmakers to experiment with multiscreen storytelling. Its success has paved the way for further exploration and innovation.

Educational Implications: The use of multiscreen storytelling in "Life of Pi" offers educators and students a rich case study in film analysis. It serves as an example of how technology can be used to teach complex narrative and visual concepts.

Future Possibilities: The success of "Life of Pi" hints at the untapped potential of multiscreen storytelling. As technology continues to evolve, so will the opportunities for filmmakers to engage audiences in novel ways.

Conclusion: "Life of Pi" is a testament to the power of multiscreen storytelling in modern cinema. Its use of this technology offers lessons in creativity, collaboration, and innovation that can inspire future generations of filmmakers.

Relevance to Modern Filmmaking: As the lines between cinema, virtual reality, and interactive media continue to blur, "Life of Pi" serves as a valuable reference point. Its pioneering use of multiscreen storytelling offers a glimpse into the future of cinematic expression, paving the way for filmmakers to push the boundaries of visual storytelling.

64

Part VI: Genre and Style

The exploration of genre and style in cinema is akin to a journey through a rich and diverse landscape of emotions, themes, and aesthetics. It is where filmmakers express their unique voices, and audiences find their resonances. In this part, we'll delve into the evolution of different genres from the hard-hitting drama of "Pulp Fiction" to the visual elegance of romance in "La La Land." Along the way, we'll also uncover the shadowy corners of Noir and Neo-Noir with examples like "Drive." Whether you're drawn to experimental cinema or high-octane action films, the chapters in this section will guide you through the multifaceted world of genre and style, showcasing how filmmakers utilize these categories to create distinct and unforgettable cinematic experiences.

The Evolution of Genre - Example: "Pulp Fiction"

Introduction to Genre Evolution

The evolution of cinematic genres reflects the transformation of society, culture, and technology. Genres not only categorize films but also shape the narrative and aesthetics, creating a shared language between filmmakers and audiences. Quentin Tarantino's 1994 classic, "Pulp Fiction," serves as an exemplary manifestation of this evolution, providing a fresh and unconventional approach to the crime genre.

Pulp Fiction's Narrative Structure

What sets "Pulp Fiction" apart is its non-linear narrative structure, a groundbreaking departure from traditional storytelling. Its interwoven plotlines challenge the viewer to piece together the storyline actively, making each viewing a unique experience.

Genre Blending in Pulp Fiction

Rather than sticking to a single genre, "Pulp Fiction" blends elements of crime, drama, comedy, and thriller. This amalgamation creates a film that defies easy categorization, reflecting the complexities and contradictions of modern life.

Character Development and Dialogue

The characters in "Pulp Fiction" are rich and multifaceted, each with their unique voice. Tarantino's dialogue is both sharp and witty, providing insight into the characters' worldviews and motivations. The famous diner scene showcases this mastery of dialogue, making it a memorable part of cinematic history.

Violence and Aesthetics

"Pulp Fiction" is noted for its stylized violence, a hallmark of Tarantino's filmmaking. The way violence is portrayed is not merely for shock value but serves a thematic purpose, contributing to the film's overall aesthetic and philosophical undertones.

Music and Soundtrack

The soundtrack of "Pulp Fiction" has become as iconic as the film itself. The carefully selected tracks add to the film's mood, character, and period authenticity, creating a seamless blend of visual and auditory experience.

Cultural Impact of Pulp Fiction

"Pulp Fiction" had a profound impact on popular culture. From the dance scene to the philosophical discussions, it introduced new norms and standards in filmmaking, inspiring a generation of filmmakers to think outside traditional genre boundaries.

Influence on Independent Filmmaking

Released at a time when independent films were gaining prominence, "Pulp Fiction" played a pivotal role in showcasing the creative possibilities outside major studios. Its success proved that innovative storytelling and genre-defying approaches could achieve both critical acclaim and commercial success.

The Legacy of Tarantino

Tarantino's influence extends beyond "Pulp Fiction." His ability to reimagine and redefine genres has left an indelible mark on cinema, encouraging filmmakers to take risks and challenge the status quo.

Impact on Crime Genre

By reimagining the crime genre, "Pulp Fiction" breathed new life into a well-established category of filmmaking. Its impact is still felt in modern crime films, which continue to draw inspiration from its innovative storytelling techniques.

Postmodernism in Pulp Fiction

"Pulp Fiction" is often cited as a postmodern film, embracing ambiguity, parody, and a self-referential style. Its complex relationship with genre is emblematic of postmodernism's multifaceted nature, making it a subject of academic interest and analysis.

The Femme Fatale and Gender Roles

The film's portrayal of women, particularly Uma Thurman's character Mia Wallace, offers a fresh take on the femme fatale archetype. The intricate exploration of gender roles within the criminal underworld adds depth to the characters and the narrative.

Global Impact and Reception

"Pulp Fiction's" impact was not limited to Hollywood; it resonated with audiences worldwide. Its blend of American pop culture with universal themes created a global phenomenon, illustrating the power of genre evolution in connecting disparate cultures.

Censorship and Controversy

The film's portrayal of violence and drug use sparked controversy and censorship in various countries. These debates continue to fuel discussions about artistic freedom, societal norms, and the responsibilities of filmmakers.

Conclusion: The Enduring Influence of Pulp Fiction

"Pulp Fiction" continues to be celebrated for its innovative storytelling, genre blending, and cultural impact. More than a film, it represents a turning point in cinema, where genre became a fluid and creative force rather than a rigid classification. Its legacy endures, inspiring filmmakers to push boundaries and audiences to expect the unexpected, a true testament to the power and evolution of genre in filmmaking.

Experimental and Independent Films - Example: "Moonlight"

Introduction to Experimental and Independent Films

Experimental and independent films often break free from conventional storytelling, providing unique voices and perspectives. Barry Jenkins' "Moonlight" (2016) stands as a testament to the power of independent cinema, with its subtle yet profound exploration of identity, sexuality, and African American experience.

Moonlight's Three-Part Structure

"Moonlight" unfolds in a three-part structure, chronicling the protagonist Chiron's life as a child, teenager, and adult. This fragmentation provides an intimate look into his evolving identity and the complex factors shaping it.

Visual Storytelling and Cinematography

The film's visual storytelling is striking, employing close-ups and color palettes to evoke emotion and convey internal struggles. Cinematographer James Laxton's work in "Moonlight" presents a new way of seeing, allowing audiences to connect deeply with the characters.

Sound and Silence in Moonlight

Sound design plays a crucial role in "Moonlight," where silence is as potent as dialogue. The auditory experience, whether through music or ambient sound, immerses the viewer in Chiron's world and emotions.

Challenges of Independent Filmmaking

"Moonlight's" success was hard-earned, reflecting the challenges and triumphs of independent filmmaking. Its modest budget and creative constraints led to innovative solutions, resulting in a rich and original cinematic experience.

LGBTQ Representation and Intersectionality

The portrayal of Chiron's sexual orientation is both nuanced and respectful. "Moonlight" adds complexity to the often one-dimensional portrayal of LGBTQ characters in cinema, especially within the African American community.

Casting and Performance

The casting in "Moonlight" is remarkable for its authenticity. Each actor playing Chiron across different life stages captures a consistent essence, providing a seamless transition between chapters and offering a deep, multifaceted portrayal.

Community and Environment

The depiction of Liberty City, Miami, transcends mere setting and becomes a character in itself. "Moonlight" explores the community's influence on individual identity and how place and people are inextricably intertwined.

Themes of Masculinity

"Moonlight" questions traditional definitions of masculinity, offering a sensitive examination of what it means to be a man. The film's exploration of vulnerability and strength within male relationships is both refreshing and thought-provoking.

Impact on Independent Cinema

"Moonlight's" commercial and critical success has had a lasting impact on the independent film landscape. Its achievements demonstrate that thoughtful, diverse, and experimental storytelling can resonate with wide audiences.

Cultural Relevance and Social Commentary

The film's exploration of race, sexuality, and socio-economic struggles makes it more than just a personal story; it's a reflection of broader societal issues. "Moonlight" has ignited important conversations about representation and inclusivity in cinema.

Awards and Recognition

"Moonlight" received widespread acclaim, culminating in the Best Picture win at the 89th Academy Awards. Its recognition on such a grand stage highlighted the importance and potential of experimental and independent films.

Influence on Filmmakers and Artists

The artistic and narrative choices in "Moonlight" have inspired filmmakers and artists to take risks and embrace unconventional storytelling techniques. Its influence is evident in a new wave of innovative cinema.

Educational Value and Study

"Moonlight" has become an essential text for film studies, with its intricate narrative, character development, and visual aesthetics. It offers rich material for analysis and exploration, contributing to the academic understanding of cinema.

Conclusion: The Enduring Legacy of Moonlight

"Moonlight" is more than a film; it's a statement about the power of empathy, art, and independent voice in cinema. Its bold storytelling, compelling characters, and thematic depth will continue to resonate, ensuring its place in the annals of film history. It stands as a beacon for aspiring filmmakers and a reminder that experimental and independent films can, indeed, reach hearts and change minds.

The Romantic Frame: Cinematography in Romance Films - Example: "La La Land"

Introduction to Romance and Cinematography in "La La Land"

"La La Land" (2016) revitalized the romance genre, infusing it with vibrant imagery and capturing the emotional essence of love. This chapter will explore the cinematography of this modern musical and its significant impact on romance films.

Visual Homage to Classical Musicals

The film pays visual homage to classical musicals, employing grand tracking shots and intricate choreography. Cinematographer Linus Sandgren used anamorphic lenses to create a nostalgic look reminiscent of the golden age of Hollywood.

Color and Emotion

Color in "La La Land" is not merely a visual tool but a narrative one. The deliberate use of specific hues conveys emotions and themes, intertwining with the characters' love story.

Music and Movement

The musical numbers in "La La Land" are brought to life through fluid camera movements and graceful framing. The choreography of both camera and actors creates an immersive, dreamlike experience.

Contrasting Realism and Fantasy

The cinematography skillfully balances the whimsical fantasy of a musical with the gritty realism of modern life. This contrast emphasizes the bittersweet nature of love and dreams.

Iconic Los Angeles Landscapes

Los Angeles becomes a character in "La La Land," with its iconic landscapes providing a picturesque backdrop for the romance. The city's lights and landscapes are captured with both intimacy and grandeur.

Innovation in Lighting

The lighting techniques in "La La Land" contribute to the film's visual charm. Whether through natural light or carefully crafted artificial setups, lighting is used to paint emotions and set the mood.

The Emotional Power of Close-ups

Close-ups in "La La Land" allow the audience to connect with the characters and their internal struggles. These shots are essential in conveying intimacy and vulnerability in the romantic narrative.

Editing and Transition

The transitions and editing in the film enhance the storytelling, seamlessly blending scenes and musical numbers. The fluidity in editing reflects the film's themes of aspiration and love.

The Final Sequence: A Cinematic Ballet

The final sequence in "La La Land" is a masterful cinematic ballet, summarizing the film's themes through a medley of scenes and songs. It encapsulates the what-ifs of romance in a visually stunning manner.

Impact on the Romance Genre

"La La Land" has left a significant imprint on the romance genre, reminding audiences of the power of love stories. Its blend of modern storytelling with classical techniques has set a new standard for romance films.

Critical Acclaim and Awards

The film received numerous awards and critical acclaim, particularly for its cinematography. This recognition showcases the importance of visual storytelling in conveying the universality of love.

Influence on Filmmakers

The success of "La La Land" has inspired filmmakers to explore and innovate within the romance genre. Its visual style and narrative depth continue to influence contemporary cinema.

Audience Connection and Cultural Impact

"La La Land" resonated with audiences worldwide, creating a cultural phenomenon. Its universal themes and captivating visuals struck a chord, solidifying its place in cinematic history.

Conclusion: The Lasting Legacy of "La La Land"

"La La Land" is more than a romance film; it's a celebration of love, dreams, and the magic of cinema. Its cinematic techniques will continue to inspire and captivate, marking it as an enduring masterpiece in the romantic genre. Its blend of creativity, emotion, and innovation leaves a lasting legacy, reaffirming the romance genre's place in contemporary filmmaking.

The Action Shot: Dynamic Cinematography in Action Films - Example: "John Wick"

Introduction to Dynamic Action Cinematography in "John Wick"

"John Wick" (2014) is renowned for its intense action sequences and masterful cinematography. The following exploration of the film's techniques showcases its innovation and impact on the action genre.

Long Takes and Seamless Action

The film employs long takes, allowing the audience to follow the fast-paced action without interruption. This choice adds to the realism and immersion, pulling viewers into John Wick's relentless world.

Choreography and Coordination

Choreography goes beyond the physical movement of characters. In "John Wick," it also involves the camera's motion, creating a dance between actor and camera that enhances the visual impact of each scene.

Gun Fu: A Stylistic Choice

The film popularized "Gun Fu," a style that blends martial arts with gunplay. This technique offers a unique visual spectacle and exemplifies the character's skill and precision.

Realistic Sound Design

Sound plays a vital role in grounding the action. The authentic sound of firearms and impacts adds to the immersion, making every shot and hit feel tangible.

Use of Practical Effects

"John Wick" favors practical effects over CGI, contributing to the tactile realism of the fight scenes. Practical effects create a visceral experience that resonates with audiences.

The Importance of Stunt Work

The collaboration between actors and stunt performers in "John Wick" is unparalleled. Keanu Reeves' commitment to performing his own stunts adds authenticity and connects the audience to the character.

Dynamic Lighting and Color Palette

Lighting and color are used to accentuate emotions and guide the viewer's focus. The film's distinctive palette enhances the action and adds depth to the visual storytelling.

Spatial Awareness and Environment

"John Wick" uses its environments creatively, turning ordinary locations into battlefields. The film's understanding of space and how to use it dynamically contributes to its unique action style.

Editing: Balancing Intensity and Clarity

The editing in "John Wick" maintains clarity while conveying the chaos of action. Quick cuts are avoided, allowing the audience to follow the action and appreciate the craftsmanship. The camera tends to follow the action, appreciating each move that is struck.

Musical Score: Enhancing Momentum

The film's soundtrack complements the on-screen action, providing rhythm and emotional context. Music becomes a driving force that carries the audience through each sequence.

Cinematic Influence and Legacy

"John Wick" has left an indelible mark on action cinema, inspiring filmmakers to approach action sequences with a new level of artistry and care.

The Birth of a Franchise

The success of "John Wick" led to the creation of a franchise, with each installment further exploring and expanding on the visual and thematic concepts introduced in the original.

Audience Impact and Cultural Resonance

"John Wick" captured the attention of audiences worldwide, resonating not only for its action but for its character-driven story. Its innovative techniques continue to influence contemporary filmmaking.

Conclusion: A New Standard for Action Cinema

"John Wick" has redefined the way action sequences are crafted, appreciated, and experienced. Its blend of dynamic cinematography, expert choreography, and emotional storytelling set a new standard for action films. By seamlessly integrating all these elements, "John Wick" offers a thrilling experience that transcends the genre and continues to inspire filmmakers and audiences alike.

Noir and Neo-Noir: Shadows and Style - Example: "Drive"

Introduction: A Bridge Between Noir and Neo-Noir

"Drive" (2011), directed by Nicolas Winding Refn, stands as a bridge between traditional noir and contemporary neo-noir cinema. It's a film that elegantly pays homage to the past while showcasing a unique and modern style, setting itself apart within the genre.

The Prototypical Noir Hero

Ryan Gosling's character, Driver, is a reflection of the prototypical noir hero. A stoic figure trapped by circumstance, he embodies the existential struggles that have long defined noir protagonists, illuminating a connection between classic and contemporary themes.

Stylistic Visual Homage to Noir

"Drive" captures the visual essence of noir through its use of shadows, reflections, and stark lighting contrasts. These techniques, nuanced and deliberate, evoke the emotional tension and moral ambiguity that characterize the genre.

Neo-Noir and the Modern Cityscape

While honoring traditional noir aesthetics, "Drive" also embraces the neon-lit urban landscapes that define neo-noir. The cinematography brings Los Angeles to life as a character itself, reflecting a world of duality and decay.

Sound and Music: An Auditory Landscape

The film's synth-heavy soundtrack, coupled with a minimalist sound design, adds a layer of atmospheric tension that resonates with the visual styling. This careful attention to sound builds a rich and immersive neo-noir experience.

Violence and Realism: A Stark Contrast

"Drive" portrays violence with both stylized and shockingly realistic tones. The juxtaposition of poetic imagery with brutal violence underscores the film's thematic complexity and emotional weight.

Character Development and Relationships

The film explores complex relationships and emotional connections that drive its narrative. These interactions reveal the characters' humanity, allowing viewers to sympathize with figures traditionally seen as morally ambiguous.

The Femme Fatale Reimagined

In "Drive," the femme fatale archetype is subtly reimagined. Carey Mulligan's character represents innocence rather than danger, challenging traditional genre conventions and contributing to the film's unique identity.

Narrative Structure and Pacing

The deliberate pacing and nonlinear narrative structure create a dreamlike quality, enhancing the film's thematic depth. This allows for a slow-burning tension that is both engaging and disconcerting, mirroring the protagonist's internal struggle.

Cinematic Influences and Tributes

"Drive" pays tribute to various cinematic influences, from classic noir to European art cinema. This amalgamation creates a unique voice that honors its predecessors while carving its path.

Cultural Impact and Reception

The film's distinctive style resonated with audiences and critics alike, contributing to a resurgence of interest in neo-noir. Its impact on contemporary cinema continues to be felt, inspiring filmmakers to explore and experiment within the genre.

A Contemporary Classic: Relevance and Resonance

"Drive" remains relevant by reflecting societal anxieties and existential questions that persist in the modern age. Its resonance lies in its ability to connect with viewers on both an intellectual and emotional level.

Legacy and Influence on Future Filmmakers

The influence of "Drive" on future filmmakers is significant. Its blend of visual aesthetics, narrative complexity, and character depth has set new standards, encouraging a generation of creators to push boundaries within the noir and neo-noir genres.

Contribution to the Evolution of the Genre

"Drive" has made a lasting contribution to the evolution of the noir genre. By blending classical and modern elements, it has expanded the boundaries of what neo-noir can be, ensuring the genre's vitality and relevance in contemporary cinema.

Conclusion: A Cinematic Milestone

"Drive" stands as a cinematic milestone in the realm of noir and neo-noir. Its meticulous attention to detail, innovative storytelling, and thematic richness make it not only a thrilling cinematic experience but also an essential study in the ongoing dialogue between past and present, shadow and light, within this enduring and evolving genre.

Part VII: Global Cinema

As we transcend the familiar landscapes of Hollywood and European cinema, we embark on a journey that takes us into the vibrant and diverse world of global cinema. This section explores the nuances of Eastern cinematic traditions, as exemplified by the thought-provoking "Parasite," and delves into the emerging voices of African and Latin filmmakers, illustrated by the powerful "City of God." By uncovering the unique storytelling techniques, cultural contexts, and visual aesthetics that shape films from various regions, we illuminate the tapestry of human experience that connects us all. This exploration of global cinema enriches our understanding of the art form, reminding us that cinema is a universal language that transcends boundaries and unites us in our shared humanity.

Eastern Perspectives - Example: "Parasite"

"Parasite" is more than just a film; it's a revelation. A profound symbol of the Eastern cinema, it reflects the intricate social structures and tensions that pervade contemporary society. South Korean director Bong Joon-ho's masterpiece encapsulates a unique blend of dark humor, thriller, and social commentary, taking the audience on a thought-provoking journey.

The film opens with the impoverished Kim family, living in a squalid basement apartment, who gradually infiltrate the lives of the wealthy Park family. Through meticulous planning and manipulation, they secure jobs within the Park household, revealing a complex interplay between social classes.

"Parasite" employs distinct visual storytelling, making use of spatial divisions to represent class disparities. The contrast between the lavish Park residence and the Kim's cramped dwelling isn't just architectural; it's a tangible embodiment of the gaping divide between the rich and poor in modern society.

The use of lighting is another standout aspect of the film. The crisp, clean lighting in the Park's home sharply contrasts with the shadowy, damp atmosphere of the Kim's abode. It symbolizes the clear divide between the two families' social statuses and emphasizes their differing worldviews.

Bong Joon-ho's direction is both subtle and striking. Through his choice of camera angles and compositions, he crafts scenes that linger in the viewer's mind. One such memorable moment is the flooding of the Kim's neighborhood, where the destructive force of water visualizes the sweeping power of societal forces.

The film's genre-defying narrative allows it to transcend traditional storytelling techniques. By skillfully weaving thriller elements with comedic touches and poignant social observations, "Parasite" defies categorization. This genre fluidity adds to the film's global appeal, resonating with audiences worldwide.

"Parasite" also delves into the psychological aspects of its characters, exploring the impact of societal pressures on personal integrity and morality. The transformation of the characters throughout the film is both horrifying and fascinating, offering an introspective look into human nature.

A remarkable feature of "Parasite" is its universal applicability. While it is firmly rooted in South Korean culture, the themes of class struggle, greed, and social inequality are globally relevant. It's this universality that has helped the film reach audiences far beyond its native country.

The film's sound design also plays a crucial role in building tension and enhancing the narrative. From the carefully chosen background music to the meticulously crafted sound effects, every auditory element in "Parasite" contributes to the immersive experience.

Bong Joon-ho's screenplay is a masterclass in storytelling. The dialogues are crisp, the plot is tightly woven, and every detail serves a purpose. "Parasite" is a lesson in how every element of a screenplay can be optimized to serve the story.

"Parasite's" impact extends beyond the silver screen. It made history as the first non-English-language film to win the Best Picture award at the Oscars, breaking barriers and opening doors for other non-Western films on the global stage.

The film's commercial success, coupled with its critical acclaim, highlights the growing influence and recognition of Eastern cinema in the global film industry. It marks a shift in the acceptance and appreciation of diverse storytelling and aesthetic sensibilities.

From a cultural perspective, "Parasite" serves as an ambassador for Korean culture. Through its global success, it has sparked interest in Korean cinema, food, language, and traditions, contributing to the international spread of the Korean Wave, or "Hallyu."

At its core, "Parasite" is an exploration of the human condition. It poses difficult questions about society, morality, and individual responsibility. Its lasting impact lies in its ability to provoke thought and inspire discussion long after the credits roll.

In conclusion, "Parasite" is not merely a film but a phenomenon. Its rich storytelling, unique visual style, and piercing social commentary make it a landmark in Eastern cinema. By reflecting societal complexities and human frailties, it transcends cultural barriers, offering a compelling glimpse into universal truths. Its success is a testament to the limitless potential of cinema to connect, challenge, and inspire audiences across the globe.

The Rise of African and Latin Cinema - Example: "City of God"

"City of God" is a poignant and visceral journey into the heart of Rio de Janeiro's favelas. This Brazilian masterpiece is not only significant as a film but also as a symbol of the broader rise of African and Latin cinema on the global stage.

Directed by Fernando Meirelles and Kátia Lund, "City of God" offers an unflinching look at the violence and poverty that pervade the city's slums. Through a rich narrative and compelling characters, the film draws the viewer into a world rarely depicted with such authenticity.

One of the standout elements of "City of God" is its groundbreaking cinematography. The filmmakers employ a handheld camera technique that adds to the raw, kinetic energy of the film. This choice serves to immerse the audience in the chaos and urgency of life in the favelas.

The narrative structure of "City of God" is both complex and engaging. By weaving multiple storylines and characters, the film provides a multifaceted view of the community. It transcends a simple crime drama and delves into deeper societal issues, such as inequality, corruption, and the loss of innocence.

At the heart of "City of God" are its characters, brought to life by a cast of mostly non-professional actors from the favelas themselves. This casting choice adds an authenticity and emotional depth that resonates strongly with audiences.

The film's soundtrack, a vibrant mix of samba, bossa nova, and other Brazilian musical styles, further enriches the storytelling. It complements the visual narrative and adds cultural texture, capturing the rhythm and spirit of Rio's urban landscape.

"City of God" has had a profound impact on global cinema, showcasing the talent and creativity of Latin American filmmakers. Its success paved the way for other films from the region to gain international recognition and acclaim.

Additionally, "City of God" played a vital role in drawing attention to African and Latin filmmakers and their unique storytelling abilities. Its success underscored the importance of diverse perspectives in cinema, demonstrating that powerful stories can emerge from any corner of the globe.

The film also sparked conversations around social issues and provided a platform for dialogue on topics such as poverty, crime, and urban development. Its unfiltered portrayal of life in the favelas spurred debates and inspired real-world initiatives to address these challenges.

"City of God" also had a lasting impact on cinematic techniques, influencing a generation of filmmakers. Its innovative use of visual storytelling, editing, and sound design has been emulated and admired by many in the industry.

Beyond its artistic accomplishments, "City of God" also represents a commercial success story for African and Latin cinema. Its international box office performance demonstrated that non-Hollywood films could achieve financial success, inspiring other filmmakers in the region to pursue their artistic visions.

The film's social and cultural significance extends to its portrayal of youth in the favelas. By humanizing and empathizing with its young characters, "City of God" challenges stereotypes and provides a nuanced understanding of their struggles and aspirations.

Furthermore, "City of God" illustrates the power of cinema as a tool for social change. It not only entertains but educates, enlightens, and encourages viewers to engage with complex social realities.

In the context of global cinema, "City of God" stands as a testament to the richness and diversity of African and Latin storytelling. Its universal themes, coupled with a distinct cultural perspective, make it a film that transcends boundaries and resonates with audiences worldwide.

In conclusion, "City of God" is more than just a film; it's a cultural phenomenon. It marked a pivotal moment in the rise of African and Latin cinema, showcasing the extraordinary talents and unique voices of these regions. Through its compelling narrative, innovative filmmaking, and social consciousness, it has left an indelible mark on the world of cinema, inspiring filmmakers and audiences alike.

Part VIII: The Future Landscape

As we cast our gaze toward the horizon of cinematography, we find a landscape brimming with innovation, creativity, and transformation. The chapters that follow in this part will explore the cutting-edge facets of modern filmmaking that are redefining the industry. From the embrace of sustainable practices and ethical considerations in "The Revenant" to the thrilling world of virtual reality exemplified by "Ready Player One," and the exciting potential of remote filming in projects like "The Midnight Sky," the future of cinema holds endless possibilities. Together, these chapters map a journey into uncharted territory, shedding light on the trends and technologies that will shape the cinematic experiences of tomorrow.

Sustainability and Ethics - Example: "The Revenant"

Introduction to Sustainability and Ethics in Filmmaking

Sustainability and ethics are not words that traditionally resonate with Hollywood. Yet, in the face of global challenges, the film industry has begun to recognize the imperative need for responsible practices. Alejandro González Iñárritu's "The Revenant" serves as a beacon, epitomizing these values. Through its production, it provides a framework for understanding how sustainability and ethics can be intertwined with filmmaking.

Setting the Scene: "The Revenant"

"The Revenant" is a story of survival, revenge, and human interaction with nature. It's not just the narrative that takes us back to the wild but also the making of the film itself. Filmed in 12 remote locations, the creators challenged themselves with ethical environmental considerations.

Environmental Consciousness in Production

From the beginning, the production team aimed for an environmentally conscious approach. They utilized solar panels, reduced carbon emissions, and worked closely with environmental consultants. This responsibility to nature echoed the movie's thematic focus on man's relationship with the environment.

Respecting Native Cultures

Respect for indigenous cultures was another ethical concern. Collaboration with Native American advisors ensured that the film depicted indigenous cultures with accuracy and dignity, avoiding stereotypes and misrepresentations.

The Challenges of Ethical Filmmaking

Sustainable and ethical filmmaking is not without challenges. The filming of "The Revenant" faced logistical hurdles, from transportation to the management of waste. Yet, these challenges were met with innovative solutions that demonstrated a commitment to ethical principles.

Natural Lighting: A Sustainable Choice

Cinematographer Emmanuel Lubezki's choice to use natural lighting was not merely an artistic decision but also a sustainable one. It minimized the use of energy-consuming lighting equipment, reducing the film's carbon footprint.

Economic Implications

Sustainable practices often come with higher upfront costs. Investing in eco-friendly materials and technology required a larger budget. However, the long-term benefits to the environment and the positive public image make it a worthy investment.

Ethical Treatment of Animals

The depiction of animals in "The Revenant" was done with careful consideration. The production team used visual effects for scenes involving animal violence, ensuring that no animals were harmed or treated unethically.

The Impact on the Film Industry

"The Revenant" set a precedent in the industry. Its success at the box office and awards proved that a film can maintain artistic integrity while upholding ethical and sustainable practices. It invites other filmmakers to take the leap.

A Message Beyond Entertainment

The film doesn't only entertain; it educates. The underlying message of respect for nature and the focus on sustainability resonate with audiences, prompting them to reflect on their relationship with the environment.

Criticism and Dialogue

Despite its efforts, "The Revenant" also faced criticism from some environmental activists. This criticism sparks a crucial dialogue within the industry, encouraging continuous improvement and transparency in sustainable practices.

Future Perspectives

The legacy of "The Revenant" extends beyond its cinematic achievements. It represents a call to action for the industry, encouraging filmmakers to adopt sustainable and ethical practices as the standard rather than the exception.

Integration with Educational Curriculum

Universities and film schools are integrating the case of "The Revenant" into their curriculum, teaching the next generation of filmmakers the importance of sustainability and ethics in the creative process.

Conclusion: A New Era of Filmmaking

"The Revenant" symbolizes a turning point in the film industry, merging artistic excellence with moral responsibility. It serves as a blueprint for the industry, proving that a commitment to sustainability and ethics can coexist with commercial and critical success.

Key Takeaways

Through the lens of "The Revenant," we can glimpse the future of filmmaking. It teaches us that films can be more than mere stories; they can be catalysts for change, embodying the values of the society they aim to entertain and inspire. It's a lesson in cinema that transcends the screen, impacting the real world and shaping a new era of responsible filmmaking.

Virtual Reality and Beyond - Example: "Ready Player One"

Introduction to the Realm of Virtual Reality

"Ready Player One" is not just a film; it's an exploration of the future of virtual reality (VR) in entertainment. Directed by Steven Spielberg, the movie dives deep into the potentials and risks of a world where VR becomes the primary escape from reality.

The Plot and Significance of "Ready Player One"

Set in a dystopian future, the film follows Wade Watts as he navigates the virtual world of the OASIS, seeking hidden treasure. The journey becomes symbolic, reflecting contemporary debates about the integration of virtual and real worlds.

VR as an Artistic Medium

"Ready Player One" showcases the power of VR as an artistic medium. Spielberg creates immersive environments that stretch the boundaries of visual storytelling, challenging traditional cinematic techniques.

Technological Innovation Behind the Scenes

The film required cutting-edge technology to render the intricate virtual world. This highlights the rapid advancements in VR technology and its increasing accessibility to filmmakers.

Exploring the Social Impact of VR

The movie delves into the social implications of VR, illustrating a world where people prefer virtual experiences to real connections. It offers a cautionary tale about the balance between technology and human interaction.

VR as a Tool for Education and Exploration

The OASIS is not merely a game; it's an educational platform. Through its depiction, the film emphasizes the potential of VR for learning and personal growth, opening doors to new educational methodologies.

The Ethical Considerations of VR

Alongside its wonders, "Ready Player One" exposes the ethical dilemmas surrounding VR, such as addiction, inequality, and control over virtual spaces. It prompts viewers to consider the moral responsibilities of a fully virtualized society.

Emphasizing Physical Limitations and Humanity

Though set in a virtual world, the film never lets viewers forget the physical limitations and real emotions of the characters. It grounds the fantastical elements in human experience, bridging the gap between the virtual and the real.

Audience Engagement through Nostalgia

With numerous pop culture references, "Ready Player One" taps into nostalgia, bridging generations and connecting viewers to the virtual journey. This clever blend of past and future enhances audience engagement.

Accessibility and Inclusivity in VR

The film also touches on the themes of accessibility and inclusivity in virtual spaces, reflecting the real-world efforts to make VR more available and accommodating to diverse users.

The Economics of Virtual Worlds

Through its fictional economy, the movie offers insight into the burgeoning field of virtual economics, reflecting the rise of cryptocurrency and digital assets in our reality.

Implications for Future Filmmaking

"Ready Player One" serves as a testament to how VR can revolutionize filmmaking. The blend of virtual environments with traditional storytelling techniques marks a new frontier in cinema.

Influence on Gaming and Entertainment Industry

The film has had a broader impact on the gaming and entertainment industries, inspiring new VR experiences and fueling interest in immersive virtual spaces.

Conclusion: A Vision of What's to Come

More than just a sci-fi adventure, "Ready Player One" offers a multifaceted exploration of virtual reality. It's a celebration of technological innovation and a reflection on the social, ethical, and artistic implications of a world where the virtual becomes indistinguishable from the real.

Key Takeaways

"Ready Player One" stands as a cultural landmark, epitomizing the potential of virtual reality in entertainment and beyond. It opens the door to endless possibilities, encouraging us to question, explore, and imagine what the future of virtual existence might entail.

Remote Filming and Global Collaboration - Example: "The Midnight Sky"

Introduction to Remote Filming

In the world of cinematography, "The Midnight Sky," directed by George Clooney, serves as an illustrative example of the burgeoning trend of remote filming and global collaboration. This film opens a discussion about the future of film production in a digitally connected world.

The Story and Symbolism of "The Midnight Sky"

The film's narrative, set in a post-apocalyptic future, intertwines with the themes of isolation and connection, reflecting the challenges and opportunities of remote collaboration in filmmaking.

Global Collaboration in Production

"The Midnight Sky" demonstrates the immense possibilities of working with talent from around the world. From actors to production teams, this movie brings together a diverse set of individuals to create a unified vision.

Technological Innovation in Remote Filming

The production used advanced technology to coordinate remote shoots and combine footage from different locations. It stands as a testament to the creative potential of modern filmmaking tools.

Challenges and Solutions in Remote Collaboration

While the global collaboration in the movie was revolutionary, it also posed unique challenges. Solutions such as synchronized workflows and virtual meetings allowed seamless integration across distances.

Environmental Considerations and Sustainability

Remote filming as seen in "The Midnight Sky" can also be an eco-conscious choice. By reducing travel and utilizing local resources, it supports sustainability within the industry.

The Role of Editing in Integrating Global Inputs

Editing played a pivotal role in synthesizing various elements from different locations. The film shows how skilled editing can make a globally distributed production feel cohesive and unified.

Cultural Sensitivity and Inclusivity in Global Filmmaking

Working with a diverse team requires understanding and respecting different cultural nuances. "The Midnight Sky" symbolizes the importance of cultural inclusivity in global filmmaking.

Impact on Talent Accessibility

Remote filming enables access to talents who might otherwise be unavailable due to geographical constraints. This broadens the creative possibilities and adds new dimensions to storytelling.

The Influence on Set Design and Location Scouting

By embracing remote collaboration, filmmakers can virtually explore and utilize various locations, adding depth and authenticity to the visual experience.

Implications for Film Budgeting

Global collaboration may lead to cost efficiency by leveraging local resources and minimizing travel expenses. It also allows for more flexible budgeting to achieve creative goals.

Legal and Regulatory Considerations

Collaborating across borders introduces legal complexities. Proper understanding and compliance with international regulations are crucial for a successful global production.

The Future of Remote Filming and Collaboration

"The Midnight Sky" is a glimpse into a future where global collaboration becomes the norm. The potential to bring together creativity and technology from around the world promises a new era of cinematic expression.

Conclusion: A Shift in Filmmaking Paradigm

The film represents a paradigm shift in how movies can be created, introducing a new way of thinking about collaboration and artistic expression. It challenges traditional filmmaking boundaries and sets a precedent for future innovations.

Key Takeaways

"The Midnight Sky" is more than a cinematic achievement; it is an emblem of the technological and creative evolution happening in the film industry. Through remote filming and global collaboration, it unveils a path for filmmakers to explore uncharted territories, fostering creativity, inclusivity, and sustainability. The practices demonstrated in this film are not merely trends but potential standard practices for the future of cinema.

Conclusion

The world of cinema is a constantly evolving art form, a narrative medium that has transformed with every technological innovation and cultural shift. From the black and white masterpieces of the Classical Hollywood era to the immersive experiences provided by virtual reality, the chapters within this book have chronicled the monumental changes in cinematography. Whether through the artistic ingenuity of the New Wave, the remarkable advances in digital technology, or the embracing of global perspectives, filmmaking continues to redefine itself. In this conclusion, we'll reflect on the comprehensive journey through film history and its artistry, looking at what these changes signify for the future of cinema.

A Forward-Looking Reflection

As we stand on the precipice of a new era in cinema, reflecting on the paths that have led us here, we can't help but be awestruck by the infinite possibilities ahead. The past century of film has seen continuous evolution, shifting paradigms, and new waves of creativity. What may seem like a distant future is closer than we think, and it's time to envision what cinema could be.

One of the most exciting prospects of the future landscape of film lies in the realms of virtual and augmented reality. While "Ready Player One" provided a glimpse of what virtual reality in cinema might look like, the true potential of immersive storytelling remains largely unexplored. We can anticipate films that not only draw the audience into the world visually but allow them to interact with the story, characters, and environment in real-time.

Alongside technological innovations, the democratization of film production is set to grow. Tools and platforms that once were only accessible to major studios are increasingly available to independent filmmakers. This is likely to give rise to a new generation of voices and stories, reflecting more diverse and authentic perspectives. Platforms like YouTube and TikTok have already shown how individual content creators can influence the mainstream, and this trend will only accelerate.

The emergence of global cinema will continue to play a vital role in shaping the art form. As we've seen in works like "Parasite," non-Western narratives are commanding international attention and breaking down barriers. The infusion of different cultural nuances, aesthetics, and storytelling techniques will enrich the global cinematic tapestry, fostering empathy and understanding across borders.

Sustainability is also poised to be a defining feature of the industry. With films like "The Revenant" setting examples for environmentally conscious production, filmmakers will increasingly incorporate green practices. Whether through the use of renewable energy, waste reduction, or digital alternatives to traditional materials, a sustainable approach to filmmaking will become both a moral imperative and an industry standard.

Storytelling itself may undergo a transformation, moving beyond conventional formats to embrace experimental and nonlinear narratives. With a growing acceptance of unconventional filmmaking, audiences will become more receptive to stories told in abstract, poetic, or metaphorical terms. This shift could unleash a new wave of creativity, allowing filmmakers to explore deeper emotional truths and human experiences.

Remote filming and collaboration, as seen in "The Midnight Sky," will also become more common, perhaps even becoming a mainstay of film production. This approach not only allows for greater flexibility and efficiency but can also create unique creative partnerships, connecting talents from different parts of the world.

The future also holds challenges, especially in navigating the balance between technological advancement and the human element of storytelling. The rise of AI and machine learning in film production could raise ethical questions and concerns about the preservation of the artist's voice. The industry must be mindful to maintain the soul and authenticity that make cinema such a powerful medium.

In the distribution landscape, we may witness further changes with streaming platforms and digital releases becoming even more prominent. This shift will alter not only how films are consumed but also how they are funded, marketed, and perceived by audiences. Understanding and adapting to these changes will be vital for filmmakers and producers alike.

Education and mentorship in the industry are likely to become more decentralized and accessible. With online courses, workshops, and communities, aspiring filmmakers from various backgrounds will have more opportunities to learn, collaborate, and grow. This democratization of knowledge will foster innovation and help in breaking down traditional barriers to entry.

Looking forward, the blending of genres may become more pronounced, reflecting a world that is increasingly interconnected and multifaceted. Genre hybrids that creatively combine elements of action, romance, comedy, and drama will offer fresh and exciting experiences, challenging conventional categorizations.

Social and political themes will continue to resonate in cinema, reflecting the zeitgeist of the times. Filmmakers will grapple with pressing global issues such as inequality, climate change, and social justice, using the medium to inspire change and provoke thought.

Lastly, the relationship between filmmakers and audiences will likely become more interactive and participatory. Crowdsourcing, feedback loops, and community-driven projects may become more common, empowering viewers to take part in the creative process and making cinema a more collaborative art form.

The future of cinema is both thrilling and unpredictable. The challenges and opportunities that lie ahead are many, but one thing is certain: the art of filmmaking will continue to evolve, surprise, and enchant us. As technology, culture, and creativity intersect in new ways, the boundaries of what is possible will expand, and we will be witnesses to the unfolding of a new cinematic era.

This reflection, while comprehensive, is but a glimpse into the myriad possibilities that await. As filmmakers, critics, and lovers of cinema, we must remain open, curious, and adaptive. The future is an unwritten script, waiting for us to breathe life into it, frame by frame. Let us embrace the unknown with excitement and forge ahead with a vision that honors the rich legacy of the past while shaping the luminous future of film.

Appendix

Glossary of Film Terms

- **Aerial Shot**: A shot taken from a crane, plane, or drone that is usually at a significant distance from the subject, providing a bird's-eye view.

- **Aperture**: The opening in the lens through which light passes to enter the camera. It controls the amount of light reaching the film or sensor.

- **Aspect Ratio**: The ratio of the width to the height of the image. Common ratios include 4:3, 16:9, and 2.35:1.

- **Blocking**: The planning and execution of the actors' movements on the set.

- **Bokeh**: The aesthetic quality of the blur in the unfocused parts of an image.

- **Cinéma Vérité**: A documentary style that emphasizes reality and spontaneity, often using handheld cameras and natural lighting.

- **Close-Up**: A shot that tightly frames an object or person, often focusing on a face or specific detail.

- **Composition**: The arrangement of visual elements within a frame, including subjects, props, lighting, and background.

- **Continuity Editing**: The practice of arranging shots to create a clear, logical, and smooth flow of events in a film.

- **Cross-Cutting**: Editing that cuts between different scenes, often to build tension or draw parallels.

- **Dolly**: A wheeled cart or similar device on which a camera is mounted to create smooth horizontal camera movements.

- **Drone Shot**: A shot taken using a remote-controlled flying device equipped with a camera.

- **Dutch Angle**: A shot in which the camera is tilted to one side, often used to convey disorientation or tension.

- **Editing**: The process of selecting, arranging, and connecting shots to form a complete film.

- **Foley**: The reproduction of sound effects added in post-production to enhance the auditory experience.

- **Frame Rate**: The number of individual frames or images shown per second during playback. Common frame rates include 24, 30, and 60 fps.

- **Gaffer**: The head of the lighting department on a film set, responsible for implementing the lighting design.

- **Genre**: A category or type of film characterized by particular styles, themes, or content, such as action, comedy, romance, etc.

- **Handheld Shot**: A shot taken with a hand-held camera, often resulting in a shaky or unstable image.

- **Juxtaposition**: The placing of two or more shots, scenes, characters, or objects side by side for contrast or comparison.

- **Long Take**: A shot that continues for a longer than usual duration without cuts, often used to build tension or provide real-time observation.

- **Montage**: A sequence of shots or images that condenses time, space, and information, often used to show the passage of time or a complex process.

- **Mise-en-Scène**: The arrangement of scenery, props, lighting, and actors within a frame, creating the visual theme or mood.

- **Neo-Noir**: A modern or contemporary take on the classic film noir style, often characterized by moral ambiguity and stylistic choices reminiscent of noir.

- **Pan**: A horizontal camera movement in which the camera moves left or right.

- **Post-Production**: The stage in filmmaking that occurs after shooting has completed, involving editing, sound design, visual effects, etc.

- **Pre-Production**: The planning phase of filmmaking, including writing, budgeting, casting, scheduling, etc.

- **Rack Focus**: Shifting focus between subjects in the foreground and background, guiding the viewer's attention.

- **Shot/Reverse Shot**: A film technique where one character is shown looking at another character, followed by a shot of the second character looking back.

- **Slow Motion**: A technique in which time appears to slow down, achieved by shooting at a higher frame rate than playback.

- **Storyboard**: A visual representation of the film's narrative, made up of drawings or images representing each shot.

- **Tracking Shot**: A shot where the camera moves alongside the subject, often following or leading them as they move.

- **Wide Shot**: A shot that shows a large part of the scene, often used to establish setting or context.

- **Zoom**: A camera technique where the focal length of the lens is adjusted to make the subject appear closer or further away.

These terms form the building blocks of cinematography, providing a shared language for filmmakers, critics, and viewers alike. Whether you're an aspiring filmmaker or simply a lover of film, understanding these concepts can enrich your appreciation of the art form.

Recommended Films for Study

The following films have been carefully curated to exemplify various aspects of cinematography, storytelling, and filmmaking techniques across different eras, cultures, and genres. They represent an essential viewing list for students of cinema, filmmakers, and cinema enthusiasts looking to deepen their understanding of the craft.

Part I: The Foundations

- **The Silent Era**: "Metropolis" (1927), "The General" (1926)

- **Introduction of Sound**: "The Jazz Singer" (1927), "All Quiet on the Western Front" (1930)

- **Color and Cinematic Expression**: "The Wizard of Oz" (1939), "Gone with the Wind" (1939)

Part II: Classical Hollywood Cinema

- **The Studio System**: "Casablanca" (1942), "Singin' in the Rain" (1952)

- **The Art of Black and White**: "Citizen Kane" (1941), "Psycho" (1960)

- The Craft of Cinematography in the Golden Age: "Sunset Boulevard" (1950), "Rebecca" (1940)

- **Lighting Techniques**: "Touch of Evil" (1958), "Double Indemnity" (1944)

- **Camera Movement and Composition**: "Gone with the Wind" (1939), "The Searchers" (1956)

Part III: The New Wave

- **European New Wave**: "Breathless" (1960), "8½" (1963)

- **Hollywood's Response**: "Easy Rider" (1969), "Bonnie and Clyde" (1967)

Part IV: Technological Transformations

- **Digital Innovation**: "Avatar" (2009), "The Social Network" (2010)

- **Modern Special Effects**: "Inception" (2010), "Mad Max: Fury Road" (2015)

Part V: The Art and Craft

- **Composition and Framing**: "The Grand Budapest Hotel" (2014), "Birdman" (2014)

- **Mastery of Lighting**: "Blade Runner 2049" (2017), "The Revenant" (2015)

- **Digital Cinematography**: "Slumdog Millionaire" (2008), "Gravity" (2013)

- **Aerial and Drone Photography**: "Skyfall" (2012), "The Wolf of Wall Street" (2013)

- **Cinematic Storytelling**: "Life of Pi" (2012), "Her" (2013)

Part VI: Genre and Style

- **The Evolution of Genre**: "Pulp Fiction" (1994), "The Shining" (1980)

- **Experimental and Independent Films**: "Moonlight" (2016), "Requiem for a Dream" (2000)

- **Romance Films**: "La La Land" (2016), "Before Sunrise" (1995)

- **Action Films**: "John Wick" (2014), "The Dark Knight" (2008)

- **Noir and Neo-Noir**: "Drive" (2011), "Chinatown" (1974)

Part VII: Global Cinema

- **Eastern Perspectives**: "Parasite" (2019), "Spirited Away" (2001)

- **African and Latin Cinema**: "City of God" (2002), "Black Panther" (2018)

Part VIII: The Future Landscape

- **Sustainability and Ethics**: "The Revenant" (2015), "An Inconvenient Truth" (2006)

- **Virtual Reality**: "Ready Player One" (2018), "The Matrix" (1999)

- **Remote Filming and Collaboration**: "The Midnight Sky" (2020), "1917" (2019)

Whether you're exploring the pioneering techniques of the silent era or the cutting-edge technology of modern cinema, these films offer invaluable insights into the world of filmmaking. Enjoy the journey through the history, art, and innovation of cinema with this comprehensive viewing guide.

Resources and Further Reading

To deepen your understanding of cinematography, film history, and the art and craft of filmmaking, the following list of resources and further reading materials has been compiled. These resources cover various aspects of filmmaking, including different eras, techniques, and global perspectives, and will provide readers with an expansive view of the cinematic landscape.

General Film Studies:

- "Film Art: An Introduction" by David Bordwell and Kristin Thompson

- "Cinema Studies: The Key Concepts" by Susan Hayward

- "Understanding Movies" by Louis Giannetti

Part I: The Foundations:

- **The Silent Era**: "Silent Film Sound" by Rick Altman

- **Introduction of Sound**: "The Sounds of Early Cinema" edited by Richard Abel and Rick Altman

- **Color and Cinematic Expression**: "Color and the Moving Image" edited by Sarah Street and Joshua Yumibe

Part II: Classical Hollywood Cinema:

- **The Studio System**: "The Studio System" by John Belton

- **Lighting Techniques**: "Painting With Light" by John Alton

- **Camera Movement**: "Cinematic Storytelling" by Jennifer Van Sijll

Part III: The New Wave:

- **European New Wave**: "French New Wave" by Chris Wiegand

- **Hollywood's Response**: "New Hollywood Cinema: An Introduction" by Geoff King

Part IV: Technological Transformations:

- **Digital Innovation**: "Digital Cinema: The Revolution in Cinematography, Post-Production, and Distribution" by Brian McKernan

- **Modern Special Effects**: "Special Effects: The History and Technique" by Richard Rickitt

Part V: The Art and Craft:

- **Composition and Framing**: "The Filmmaker's Eye" by Gustavo Mercado

- **Mastery of Lighting**: "Light: Science and Magic" by Fil Hunter, Steven Biver, and Paul Fuqua

- **Aerial and Drone Photography**: "Aerial Photography and Videography Using Drones" by Eric Cheng

Part VI: Genre and Style:

- **Noir and Neo-Noir**: "Film Noir: An Encyclopedic Reference" by Alain Silver and Elizabeth Ward

Part VII: Global Cinema:

- **Eastern Perspectives**: "Asian Cinemas: A Reader and Guide" edited by Dimitris Eleftheriotis and Gary Needham

- **African and Latin Cinema**: "New African Cinema" by Valérie K. Orlando; "New Latin American Cinema" edited by Michael T. Martin

Part VIII: The Future Landscape:

- **Virtual Reality**: "Virtual Reality Filmmaking" by Celine Tricart

- **Sustainability and Ethics**: "Eco-Cinema Studies: The Field" by Salma Monani and Steve Rust

Online Resources:

- **Internet Movie Database (IMDb)**: A comprehensive database of film information and reviews.

- **American Society of Cinematographers (ASC)**: A professional organization that offers resources and insights from industry professionals.

- **Film Studies for Free**: An online repository of scholarly works, essays, and video essays on various aspects of cinema.

These resources serve as a foundational guide for students, filmmakers, and scholars looking to explore further the world of cinema from its early beginnings to its future innovations. Whether your interest lies in the history, aesthetics, or technology of film, this curated list will guide you in your exploration of the ever-changing canvas of cinematography.

www.ingramcontent.com/pod-product-compliance
Lightning Source LLC
Chambersburg PA
CBHW031349060726
47590CB00007B/2703